THE
SECRET
WORLD
OF KIDS

Books by

ART LINKLETTER

People Are Funny
Kids Say the Darndest Things!
The Secret World of Kids

THE
SECRET
WORLD
OF KIDS

BY Art Linkletter

Illustrated by LOUIS GLANZMAN

PUBLISHED BY
BERNARD GEIS ASSOCIATES
DISTRIBUTED BY RANDOM HOUSE

Designed by Bevans, Marks & Barrow, Inc.

Manufactured in the United States of America by American Book-
Stratford Press, New York

Paper by Royal Paper Corporation of New York

Dedication

EVERYONE LOVES the old fairy-tale ending: "And so they were married and lived happily ever after." But in my opinion the best part of any true-life story only *begins* with these words.

Certainly life's greatest challenge is raising a family. My own life has been exciting, rich and immensely rewarding in every way. I have been lucky enough to win fame and fortune beyond my dreams. And yet, the greatest and most satisfying success by far that I have enjoyed lies in my children. Helping them, watching them grow, has been my greatest joy and privilege.

My five "Links" represent what I'd like America to remember about me. And so I dedicate this book to every parent who feels, as I do, that to have a good family and bring up fine children is the most wonderful career that any man or woman can ever hope for—or ever have.

ART LINKLETTER

Acknowledgments

DURING THESE PAST fourteen years on the CBS House Party program, I have accumulated a monumental debt of gratitude to:

The 14,560 children I have interviewed on radio and television . . .

Their 29,120 parents, who trembled while they talked . . .

Their 1,789,354 cousins, their uncles and their aunts . . .

Their 58,240 grandparents . . .

The teachers who excused the 14,560 children from school.

And my heartfelt thanks also go to:

My own expert adviser on children, Dorothea Gillespie, who is on loan to me from the Los Angeles Board of Education and who escorts every child from school, takes them on a tour of the CBS studios and introduces them to me before air time. . . .

Arthur Gordon, who provided great editorial assistance, working with my editor and publisher, Bernard Geis, who in turn toiled under the watchful eye of his beautiful wife, Darlene. . . .

My wife, Lois, who gets full credit for prodding my memory and curbing my extravagances in writing of our Links. . . .

The five little Linkletters, some of whom are no longer so little but all of whom are responsible for a great deal of the raw material in this book . . .

Reuben Klamer, director of the Link Research Corporation, who served as my seeing eye for the chapter on toys and games. . . .

My own private secretary, Lee Ray, who recorded

for posterity many of the amusing and surprising remarks made by the small fry during my television interviews. . . .

And, finally, I would like to express my deepest gratitude and sincere appreciation to the thousands of letter writers, fans and viewers who have made all of this possible by encouraging me to continue my work with children both on and off the air. Your comments and criticisms have guided me in this work more than I can ever say.

ART LINKLETTER

Foreword

YOU KNOW WHAT I THINK about forewords? I think the same thing you do—I think they should be short. So let's get right down to business.

Why am I writing another book about kids? Several reasons. The deepest one, probably, is that I was an adopted child, an only child, and while my middle-aged foster parents were kind and decent people, there was no great warmth or closeness between us. I think all kids deserve such warmth and understanding from their parents. I would like to help them get it if I can.

Another reason for this book is that kids have brought so much pleasure into my own life that I like to share it. As you read these pages, I hope I'll be sharing it with you.

Still another reason is that everybody loves to give advice. I'm no exception. And when it comes to kids, I honestly think I've had more experience than most. Five of my own; I've watched them grow and change and develop over the past twenty-odd years. Fifteen thousand or so that were mine, in a sense, while I interviewed them on the air. So I have quite a few ideas about kids: what makes them happy, what makes them sad, what makes them tick.

I have a notion, too, that some parents don't have as much fun with their kids as they should. They love them, they want to help them, they'd do anything for them. But somehow they aren't as close to them as they might be. Sometimes they almost ignore their children. Sometimes they make such a production out of raising them that half the fun is lost. Some people I know seem baffled by their kids. A few act as if they were actually afraid of their own children. And so they're missing out on one of the most rewarding of all pleasures—the sheer enjoyment of being parents.

To me, raising kids is just about the most exciting, maddening, rewarding, exhausting, puzzling and satisfying occupation there is. There's no foolproof system, because all kids are different. But there's no area in the world where loving common sense and a touch of humor pay such big dividends. That's what I hope this book will be full of: fun and loving common sense.

Last time, in Kids Say the Darndest Things, I let the children do most of the talking. We'll let them have their say this time, too, but I want to chime in occasionally myself. It's an awful strain for a Linkletter to sit around and let other people do all the talking.

Kids not only say the darndest things, they sometimes pray the darndest things. Like the little boy who patterned his prayer on what he thought he heard in church. "And forgive us our trashbaskets," he prayed fervently, "as we forgive those who put trash in our baskets!"

Here's hoping the following words of wisdom don't wind up as trash in your basket. If they do, I'll never forgive myself. Or you!

ART LINKLETTER

Contents

THE
SECRET
WORLD
OF KIDS

Chapter 1
Our Kids—and Yours

Do CHILDREN REALLY LIVE in a secret world of their own, a world that grown-ups once knew but can never quite find again? Sure they do! Every parent knows this, every teacher, every grown-up who has anything to do with kids.

It's a strange and wonderful world, half fantasy, half reality. The weather there is sunny, mostly, but now and then there are storms. There's love in that world, and selfishness, and a surprising amount of violence, and sometimes fear. There's logic, too, although it gets oddly twisted at times. And magic. And more imagination than Jules Verne or Walt Disney ever dreamed of. And humor that any professional comedian would give his whole stable of gag-writers for.

It's a world where nothing is predictable and nothing is commonplace because everything is fresh and unexpected and new. You can't describe it in so many words. You have to listen for it, and watch for it.

It's a four-year-old being given a lime lollipop, and putting it aside after a thoughtful lick. "This one's green," she says. "It'll be all right when it gets ripe."

It's a runaway two-year-old who, when he sees his mother coming to snatch him away from his new-found playmates, starts jumping up and down and screaming, "This ain't me, Mommie! This ain't me!"

It's a dreamy eight-year-old writing in her diary: "Summer is a long, wide beach with a rocking chair at the end. Winter is a blue room with a lighted candle."

It's a pair of obstreperous crew-cuts having a water-pistol fight and reassuring Mother: "Don't worry, Mom; we won't get water on anything. We're using ink!"

It's an earnest seven-year-old tacking a practical P.S. onto his prayers. "And by the way, God, if I should meet a snake, will You please fix it so that I can run faster than the snake?"

It's all these things and a million more happening every minute of every day in every place on the planet that's lucky enough to be inhabited by kids.

Can grown-ups visit this secret world? I think they can. You don't need a passport or a visa or a formal invitation. All you need is a genuine love of kids and a little patience and understanding.

I think it also helps if you realize that there *are* two worlds. Some grown-ups insist on treating children as if they were small, not-very-bright adults. This is a mistake, because kids *aren't* grown-ups—they're kids.

They think and feel and talk and act in their own special way. At every successive stage, they have their own language, their own hopes and fears, their own reasons for behaving as they do.

And these are seldom grown-up reasons. Take, for example, a two-year-old busily engaged in reducing his toy sailboat to fragments which he then delightedly flushes down the toilet. This is certainly not the treatment that the sailboat was designed for, and it is likely to give the toilet acute indigestion. But the two-year-old isn't being malicious or destructive. He's merely carrying out a fascinating experiment designed to test the law of cause and effect which *you* take for granted but which is quite a novelty in his small world.

Or you surprise a four-year-old in the kitchen with cookie crumbs all over his face and jump to the conclusion (entirely correct) that he has been raiding the cookie-jar. Does he admit his guilt with proper penitence? Certainly not. He tells you blandly that a mouse did it. Does this make him a liar as well as a thief? Not unless you judge him by the standards of *your* world, which would be pretty silly. In *his* world, he's merely a kid who (a) likes cookies, (b) dislikes scoldings, (c) has enough imagination to invent an un-punishable culprit (the mouse), and (d) is doing his small best to smooth over an awkward situation.

What I hope to do in this book, if you will stick with me, is build a few bridges from one world to the other. It's the old story of setting up a line of communication, but I'm convinced that that's what it takes for parents really to enjoy their kids. I'll be speaking, not as an educator or a psychologist (which I'm not), but simply as the father of five lively youngsters of my own, as the interviewer of thousands of kids all over the world, and as a pretty serious student of that wonderful, wacky, secret world of kids.

My plan is simple, too. I'm going to introduce my own kids, and use them now and then as illustrations of some of the points I hope to make. I'm going to try to answer some of the questions that parents ask me constantly, either in person or through the mails. I'm going to pass along some of the things Lois and I think we've learned in twenty-odd hectic years of parenthood (believe me, we're still learning!). Whenever I remember an episode that proves that kids can be fun, I'm going to tell you about it. . . .

In short, I'm just going to talk about the secret world of kids as I see it every day through the most wonderful window in the world—the eyes of a child.

What's a Family For?

WHAT'S THE OLDEST INSTITUTION in the world? It's the family, isn't it? The eternal triangle consisting of Mom and Dad and the kids. This is the framework in which every one of us got started; the mold that took the raw material of heredity and made us what we are. It's the fundamental human relationship; everything is based on it, including civilization.

Cynics may argue that what holds a family together is simple necessity: man needs woman, woman needs man, kids have to be protected and fed and cared for until they can fend for themselves. But I think that most people would agree that a family ought to be a lot more than a collection of mutual needs. It ought to be fun. It ought to be a great adventure in living: exciting, stimulating, challenging. It ought to be an endless process of growth and sharing, a tremendous experiment in love.

I feel strongly about this, because as a small child I didn't have much in the way of a family. When I was only a few months old, my natural parents put me up for adoption. I have no recollection of them at all.

My foster parents, John and Mary Linkletter, were in their late forties when they adopted me. They had no children of their own, so I became—automatically—an only child.

All this happened back in 1912, in Moose Jaw, Saskatchewan—the western part of Canada. My foster father was an insurance salesman at the time, but the burning interest of his life was religion. He believed in the Bible literally, word for word. He considered everyone in the world his brother. He was full of piety and goodness, but actually he was too busy saving the world to worry very much about his own or his family's welfare. He had a serene conviction that no matter what happened, the Lord would provide. Looking back now, I must admit that the Lord always did. But sometimes it was close. . . .

My foster father had only one leg, which meant that there were no hikes or sports or the rough-and-tumble play that most boys enjoy with their dads. But I don't think that we'd have had that kind of companionship anyway. His main occupations, when he was home, were praying and reading the Bible. He made me read the Book too—often aloud. I didn't enjoy this, but I think now that it gave me an ear for words and their rhythm that has helped me enormously in my work. And, of course, it gave me whatever I possess of the religious philosophy of the greatest Book in the world.

My father was a remarkable person in many ways, but he had no common sense when it came to the harsh realities of life and no real understanding of kids. His saintliness used to cause me acute embarrassment at times. We might be walking down a street somewhere, and my father would decide that he'd like to visit some church on the other side of town. Then he'd discover that he had no carfare. So he'd walk right up to the first person we met.

"Brother," he would say, "could you spare us a little money, please?"

He saw nothing odd in such a request. If he had had a dollar of his own, he would have given it gladly to anyone who asked for it. But episodes like these used to make me want to sink through the pavement. I still grow hot inside, just thinking about them!

When I was about seven, we settled in San Diego. Even then, we moved constantly from one part of the city to another. We lived behind shoe shops (my foster father was also a cobbler, of sorts), in dingy walk-ups, at the back of stores. Once my mother and I even lived in a home for the aged. I remember that all the houses we lived in had half-numbers; we never had a full number on the door.

Living on the ragged edge of poverty didn't bother me too much; kids have a way of taking their surroundings for granted. What did bother me was the fact that I was rather small, and showed little early promise of becoming the athlete I yearned to be. But I think certain traits are born in a child, not acquired. Competitiveness is one of these, and I had my share of that. I got a paper route and earned a little money through various other chores. But I always turned my earnings over to my mother. There was never any spare cash in our household for ice cream cones or movies or the small luxuries and treats that most kids take for granted.

And so, while I was never actually hungry or neglected, my childhood was a little austere and a little lonely.

I'm describing it briefly here because there's no doubt in my mind that the absence of a normal home life acted on me as a spur. Some children might have become withdrawn or solitary. In my case, the result was just the opposite. I wanted to go places, meet people, make money, achieve security, find warmth and companionship and love.

I've been very lucky: I found all these things.

The biggest thing in my life, of course, was finding Lois. She was only sixteen when I met her, a high-school student. It was at a fraternity dance; she was wearing a sequined jacket not half as bright as her eyes. But I knew from the start that some day I would marry her, and on Thanksgiving Day in 1936, I did.

I'll tell you more about Lois as we go along. Right now, in what's left of this first chapter, I want to introduce you to the five most important results of our marriage. Before I married Lois, in the days when I spent every possible minute on the basketball court, I remember telling my college friends that when it came to having children we were going to have enough for a basketball team. Actually we did: boy, girl, boy, girl, girl. And since these five have taught me most of what I know about kids, let me present them briefly. They'll keep popping up all through this book.

Five Links in the Family Chain

LET'S START WITH THE ONE who showed up first: Jack. He was born in San Francisco in 1937. That was the year when I'd been made radio director of the San Francisco World's Fair at the earth-shaking salary of seventy-five dollars a week. We named him Arthur Jack Linkletter, but always called him Jack. We wanted our first-born to be an individual in his own right, not a chip off the old block-buster. And he was, right from the start.

Jack was brought up entirely by us. We had no money for nurses or baby-sitters; he was our do-it-yourself baby. Like all young parents, we fussed over him too much, worried about every scratch or sniffle, wondered fearfully if our inexperience would leave him warped for life. We needn't have worried. Like all kids, Jack was born with certain built-in characteristics that a bull-dozer couldn't change—let alone a parent. He was a bright, inquisitive, alert, aggressive youngster, full of beans and energy and enthusiasm. He was so

23

well-adjusted that he spoiled us, really—we thought all kids were like that!

Oh, he had his faults, all right. He had an explosive temper. I remember it took both of us to hold him when it came to a crisis like washing his hair. And he never seemed to stick to anything for more than five minutes. Brother, what a hobby-switcher he was!

First he was a stamp collector. Then it was foreign money (he still loves money—any kind!). Then it was bongo drums; he got an authentic pair, loaned the drums to a friend, couldn't remember who it was.

After the drums, it was either a harmonica or an accordion, I forget which. Anyway, it was a fancy contraption with gadgets and buttons and lights. He bought books on how to play it. Even practiced a bit. Then he lost interest, and now can't remember what happened to it.

Next he became fascinated by snakes. He bought several at school, brought them home, put them in the garage with a piece of heavy glass over the box. He was afraid to lift the glass to feed them, so Lois had to do it. The laundress was afraid to go out of the house for fear the snakes might be loose. Jack tried to sell the snakes and couldn't. So he found the name and address of a U.C.L.A. herpetologist, took the snakes over to the man's house and left them on the porch with a note asking him to be kind to the poor homeless things.

Then there was skin diving. Jack finally assembled two complete sets of tanks, spears and fins. Then he decided to make a rubber suit. Bought yards of green rubber, cut out patterns on the floor, got rubber cement, put it all together. It leaked. Saved money and bought another one. Bought the best aqualung available. It wound up sitting in the garage.

Golf? Borrowed clubs. Then bought a few. Then in England had a special set made to order—big leather case, wheeled carrier, and so on. Hasn't played since.

Music? Stereophonic sound. Recording machine. Speakers all over the house. Records, tapes and so forth. It's sitting in his new house, disconnected.

Babies? Got a brand new baby son named Michael. Diapers, bottles, cribs and so forth. Still in use.

Jack was our first and most determined money-hoarder. Some people are currency pack-rats. If they see money, they have to take it and hide it. As a little boy, Jack kept bottles and jars of pennies hidden around the place. Now he keeps 'em hidden around his own house. Never spent a nickel if he could help it.

His romantic life was like his hobbies (until he met Bobby, the girl he married). He was always going overboard for one girl after another, monopolizing each one completely for a month or six weeks, then dropping her with a dull thud. She was always the girl he was going to marry, and then—curtains! One year he cut notches underneath the mantelpiece of his room for each "love" of his life. I counted them again, just the other day. Sixteen.

All through childhood and adolescence, Jack had a

quick, fiery temper. He would lash out in a fury, then cool off and wonder why everybody was upset. I remember one time when the two of us were out walking with my mother. Two young punks running down the street jostled my mother a bit. Jack caught one and smashed him right in the face.

Another time he thought a man had stolen his wallet. Jack grabbed him by the lapels and swung him around a couple of times. Now, if you get into a scrap, and your father is something of a celebrity, it's amazing how many things can suddenly go wrong with your opponent. Jack was haled into court by the victim who claimed every sort of injury from a dislocated back to permanent damage to his nervous system. We finally got the thing straightened out, but it gave Jack quite a fright, and really cured him of his temper. He decided that if it was a choice between his temper and all those jars of money he had hidden around the house, he'd better give up his temper!

But parents can turn mistakes and mishaps to advantage. I used that occasion to make Jack see that the limelight, while pleasant and profitable, brings an extra responsibility to the people who bask in it. If the public gives you praise and recognition and money, you owe it to the people and to yourself to keep your standards high and your skirts clean.

As I write these words, Jack has graduated from college and is starting his own television show. I think he will be a success as a master of ceremonies. Partly because Jack has already had a good deal of TV experience pinch-hitting for me. Partly because he has the assurance and genuine interest in people that a successful emcee must have.

In a sense, perhaps, from now on he will be competing with me in my own profession, but this doesn't bother either of us. If I ever have to move over and make room for somebody, I can't think of anyone I'd rather make room for than Arthur Jack Linkletter.

Our Ex-Shrinking Violet

IN MANY WAYS, the second Link in our family chain was the exact opposite of Jack. Watching Dawn grow up has been a fascinating business because she's a perfect illustration of the fact that you never can tell how a child's going to turn out. They may have a whole set of characteristics through childhood and early adolescence, then make a complete about-face and exhibit all the qualities you thought they'd never have.

As a small child, Dawn was timid, shy, fearful. She was afraid to have the bathroom door shut—thought she might get locked in. She was afraid to flush the toilet—I guess she thought she might disappear herself! She was afraid of strangers. When she was a tiny baby, she was even afraid of me. If I went near her, or picked her up, she started screaming. Nobody could go near her except her mother and her nurse.

We've wondered since if this timidity might have been caused by the fact that her eyes were not focusing properly. At the age of two, we put glasses on her to correct a muscle deficiency. We thought we'd have a terrible time keeping them on her. But she was so glad to have them that she never lost them, broke them, or took them off. Corrective exercises improved her eyes to the point where she never wears glasses now. But the whole thing made us aware that sometimes there are hidden reasons for a child's behavior—and it's up to the parents to keep searching until they find them.

Dawn learned to read early, before she was in first grade. I can see her now, glued to a book, with a patch (part of the corrective exercise business) over one eye. She developed into a fast reader, loves to read, and has read many books.

We tried to combat her timidity in many ways. She was frightened to death of dogs. We'd be walking down the street, and suddenly I would find Dawn scrambling up my back, screaming and hanging onto my ears, all because she had seen a dog. Any dog, large or small, asleep or awake! So we got King, a collie puppy a month old, and gave it to Dawn for her own. Weeks passed before she would even touch it. But gradually, in learning to love it and care for it, she got over her fear of dogs. King lived with us for fifteen years, and it was a sad day for all of us when he died—still Dawn's dog.

Dawn never went in for hobbies the way Jack did. She doesn't, to this day, care about sewing, knitting, cleaning or domestic things. This was odd, in a way, because Dawn deeply wanted her mother's admiration and approval, and Lois is a whiz at hand-skills. Unlike Jack, too, Dawn never cared about money. Never saved any, never cared about making any. For a while I paid her to keep my scrap-books up to date. But money just doesn't interest her. Once she got to college with an allowance of her own, she learned to manage it better. Her worst fault—one that almost drove her tidy mother crazy—was a total inability to hang up her things or take care of clothes or possessions. In our family, if something was lost, wrinkled, crumpled or missing, Dawn was the culprit.

Despite all these gloomy facts, I'm happy to say that somewhere in her middle teens, a great sea-change came over Dawn. From a shy, timid introvert, she changed to a happy, gay, enthusiastic extrovert. As a tiny girl, she never had any enthusiasm for toys, or gifts, or parties. She always anticipated getting the worst of everything, of being left out of games, of being given the smallest piece of pie. Now she's highly appreciative, interested in everything, with a winning smile and a trick of batting her eyelashes that members of the opposite sex find interesting.

She's a wonderful dancer. I began teaching her when she was twelve, and she's always been an excellent ballroom partner. Like the rest of the Links, she's a first-class swimmer. The shy little shrinking violet we once had is completely gone.

I think the big change in Dawn really started when she went away to boarding school and learned for the first time how lucky she was to be part of a family as close-knit as ours. In the school were girls whose parents were separated or divorced, girls who saw little of their families—and sometimes didn't like what they saw, girls who were restless and rootless and unhappy. Dawn began to see that everyone doesn't have the fun and companionship that she had been taking for granted. I think this discovery, more than anything else, drew her out of herself and started her on a new track.

When the time came for college, Dawn found that most of her friends were going to universities in the East. She decided to pick a college nearer home, partly because she wanted to be near her family, partly because she wanted to meet fellows who would probably make their homes in the West. She promptly met one who became the first really big romance of her life. They were married this fall, and I see no reason why they shouldn't live happily ever after.

The lesson that Dawn taught us is plain enough: don't be too discouraged about your children's early development, or give up on them too easily. Sometimes the qualities you hope for are there all along. They'll appear when they're ready to appear, and not before. You can't force them. You just have to do the best you can—and wait.

Young Man in the Middle

BELOW JACK AND DAWN and above Sharon and Diane—in other words, right square in the middle —comes Robert. He was the best baby in the family: a blond, curly-haired, brown-eyed angel. He was always sweet-tempered, loved his baby sister Sharon, was loved by Dawn and Jack, and was never bad.

He was sensitive, though. As a small child, Robert never wanted anything but his family. He hated to go to kids' parties, school, or anywhere the family wasn't. I had to sit through hundreds of birthday parties, kindergarten plays, and so forth, because Robert wouldn't stay otherwise—and Lois wouldn't stay either, because she didn't want Robert to look like a mama's boy.

It was quite a problem. Robert would get sick—physically sick—when we left him at school. The school nurse would call, and we'd have to go and get him. There was nothing wrong with him physically; it was all emotional. Finally we had to put Sharon in nursery school so that Robert would stay in first grade. As a result, Sharon has been a year ahead of herself ever since.

Like Dawn, Robert was always afraid of dogs. (The reason for revealing all these small family skeletons, believe me, is not because I like to rattle them. It's because I want to make it clear that, like families everywhere, we had our problems and peculiarities to struggle with. The thing to remember is that struggling with 'em draws the family together.) We never did fully understand this fear, either in Dawn's case or in Robert's. Neither of them was ever bitten or attacked or molested by a dog in any way. In Robert's case, as in Dawn's, we solved the problem by keeping dogs around the house until he outgrew his dread of them.

Unlike his dad, Robert has great skill with his hands. He's always building things: model ships, guns, trains, and so on. He can open a box containing ten thousand tiny parts—and directions that would baffle a graduate of M.I.T.—and by dinner time have the whole thing assembled. In the same amount of time, I would still be trying to get the box open.

Like his mother, he's very artistic, wraps packages in unusual decorative ways, designs colorful cards for special occasions. Once, for a table decoration, he built a whole series of forts made of tiny marshmallows arranged on mirrors, dyed different colors and festooned with small flags.

He's the rock 'n roller of the gang; has won cups and prizes. Already likes girls: he's only fourteen at this writing, but is over six feet tall, and big. For his age and size, Robert is the best swimmer in the family—at least for speed events.

Jack hoarded money; Dawn didn't care about it; Robert spends it faster than it's printed. Never has a nickel; he's a compulsive spender. When he sees something he likes, he's *got* to have it—even if it means borrowing money from the cook. It never occurs to him that something better might come along.

When he's panting for a war surplus machete, or a guitar, or books on magic, he usually manages to make money somehow or other . . . selling Lois's cherished flowers to passers-by, posing for tourists at a dime per snapshot (until his dad catches him), washing cars, fixing things. He's the official fixer of the family: wires, plumbing, machinery. Fabricates mountains, villages, and so on for the annual Christmas electric train. He's a natural scrounger and scavenger: most of the surplus lumber for miles around turns up in our backyard, and often has to be taken back (under my supervision) because it really isn't so surplus.

Robert doesn't go out and make friends; he waits for them to come to him. He loves to go on family pack trips in the mountains where he invariably has nightmares and scares the rest of the Links to death with weird cries, sleep-walkings, and frights occasioned by imaginary grizzly bears and mountain lions.

He's at the age right now where he resents authority, but still needs some. He likes music, and has stuck to guitar playing and singing, but has no special ambition as yet. He's both attracted and repelled by the glamor of show business: he dislikes the publicity that inevitably follows an entertainer's family. If Robert could change his name from Linkletter to Jones, he probably would.

He's still got a lot of growing to do, but he's doing it fast. In many ways, so far, he's been the most challenging of the Links to handle. But he may surprise all of us, one of these days.

Some Are Born Wise

Two YEARS BEHIND ROBERT, and two ahead of Diane, comes Sharon, possibly the best balanced member of our whole tribe. From the start she was a self-sufficient child. Dressed herself earlier than the others, fed herself, wanted to do everything by herself, from brushing her hair to tying her shoe-laces.

A protective sort of child with no jealousy in her. When Diane was born, Sharon started right in doing things for the baby, trying to help make formulas, wash bottles, and so on. A strong maternal instinct at work here.

But she's also an adventurous kid, nothing timid about her. Before she could walk, we had her in the swimming pool in a tiny life jacket. One day she noticed Robert swimming without a jacket, so she wriggled out of hers—and promptly went straight to the bottom. I dived in and fished her out. She cried, but it was with frustration, not fear. She was annoyed with herself because she hadn't stayed up. Before the day was out, with a little help from me, she was swimming a bit. She never wore the life-jacket again. She was swimming well within a week, and has been a mermaid ever since.

Like Jack and Diane, Sharon's a money-saver, has piggy-banks loaded with odd change. She spends it wisely; not stingy, but careful. Loves to buy Christmas and birthday presents for everyone. Has a love bird in her room that she's cherished for years. Takes good care of it.

Unlike Robert, Sharon is a joiner. She likes to belong to clubs, choirs, drama classes, and so on. She's the only Link to choose a musical instrument—the piano—and stick to it faithfully. She practices cheerfully, year after year. Shows no signs of becoming a female Paderewski, but she enjoys the disciplines and mathematical patterns of music, and plays a real nice child's-recital-type piano.

Sharon can knit, sew, and do domestic things. She can even weave a little on her small hand-loom that's a lot like her mother's big one. She'll probably enjoy cooking some day—the only Link woman who ever will.

She's the only Link ever to be lost on one of our expeditions. One crowded Sunday we were at the Los Angeles zoo. With five to keep track of, and a hundred attractions to lure them away, we lost Sharon. While we were searching frantically everywhere, she calmly went to the information booth and explained her situation. Soon the public address system was calling us to come and get her. She wasn't half as upset as we were.

Sharon's a good outdoor girl. When she was nine we took her on a pack trip in the high Sierras. She rode horseback over peaks 11,000 feet high, fished for trout, hiked over glaciers, slept under the stars, and loved every minute of it.

Those trips, incidentally, are great for our family: we get away from all the pressure and tension. There's nothing to do at night: no television, no radio, no newspapers, no telephone calls. You sit around the campfire and talk, share problems, laugh over the events of the day where somebody fell in a stream, or rolled off a horse. There are chores for everybody, each chore enabling one person to help the others. It's great.

I know that most people can't do anything so elaborate for a vacation. But if a family can go somewhere together and spend a week or two "away from it all," it smoothes out a lot of wrinkles and binds the family into a closer unity.

Sharon has some acting talent, I think. With Liza Minelli (Judy Garland's daughter), she has staged many a show in our living room, often in Gay Ninety costume, or prince and princess regalia.

A very solid citizen, this Sharon of ours. Never temperamental. Never out of sorts. Some young fellow is going to get himself a wonderful wife some day. But I'm in no hurry for it to happen!

And Then There Was One

WHEN DIANE WAS BORN, ten years ago, Lois and I thought we'd created a cute pollywog: all big eyes. She's been the baby of the family: cuddled, coddled, and pampered all her life. She's not spoiled, but she's the temperamental one—all ecstasy one moment, all sadness the next. She can look like a woodsprite up to some delicious mischief, then a sad, lost look will sweep across her face, and all the bitterness and the tragedy of the world are mirrored there.

She's the champion jig-saw puzzler of the family. She started putting puzzles together when she was three, and she's still at it. She's very neat (unlike

Dawn!)—saves everything and has a place for it. Her room is tiny, and she likes it that way, not much bigger than a closet. In it she has dozens of gadgets, boxes, mobiles, dolls, and knick-knacks—each one in its proper place.

Diane's the "finder" of the family. We hardly ever go for a walk that she doesn't pick up some money, or a pretty little button, or something nice that someone has lost.

She's another ferocious money-saver—won't spend a dime.

She's the flirt of the family, using those big eyes to win over any boy who comes within range. Very affectionate—an eager kisser. Weeps over trifles, gets mad over imaginary things, forgives quickly and forgets.

Life to her is a big, bright, sunny day with occasional small black clouds scudding across the sky, intermittently bringing showers, rainbows, hail, thunderclaps, and dizzy dust-devils.

The high point of Diane's life so far was being ring-bearer at Jack's and Bobby's wedding. She carried a pillow with the double rings and watched to see that every move, every line, every detail of the ceremony was carried out correctly. If necessary, she could have performed the ritual at the drop of a minister. She still refers to herself as the "ring burier."

Of all the Links, Diane was the youngest to turn up with a sweetheart. She's had boy friends since she was five. She's a great romanticist. When she was eight, she said wistfully, "Mother, do you think it's just Fate when you meet the man you marry?" And again, at nine, "Do you think the little boy I like now might be the man I marry when I grow up?"

With all this intensity, it wouldn't surprise me if

Diane turned out to be an actress. She has great emotional range. She dramatizes everything. Last Christmas someone gave the younger children a Shirley Temple Theatre Set. One person holds a magnet under a cardboard stage and moves the little magnetic figures around. Another person reads the dialogue from a book. Sharon moved the characters, and Diane did the reading. I happened to overhear her, and I was really amazed—she read like a trained actress. She's only ten, but she already has the intonation, and the timing.

I can hardly wait for her to grow up and start supporting us all!

In Short. . . .

SO THERE THEY ARE, my five teachers in the slippery art of raising kids. I think big families are fun, and I think children born into them are lucky. Because a big family is the best training ground in the world for kids. They have to learn give-and-take, they have to learn unselfishness, they have to learn to get along with people.

More important, in a big family, the kids are constantly surrounded by love. And it's a balanced kind of love. Sometimes, in a small family, I think parental affection can be too concentrated for a child's good. In a large family, this isn't so likely to happen. The child is loved by more people, and gives his love to more, and over-intense relationships aren't so likely to develop.

Of course, the more people there are, the more relationships there are, and the more complicated family life becomes. But living is a complicated business, and the sooner kids realize it the better.

If in our big Hollywood family we've had a little more happiness and achieved a little more closeness than is sometimes the case, I honestly feel that it's largely due to the conviction Lois and I have shared from the start—that kids are loaned to us by life for a certain number of years primarily to be loved and enjoyed.

We've had our problems, Heaven knows, and moments of discouragement. But really, that's part of the fun. Without problems life would be pretty dull, wouldn't it? You certainly wouldn't learn much.

If you want to know some of the things we've learned, just turn the page and keep reading—that's all!

Chapter 2

How to Bend a Twig

KIDS ARE PRETTY WONDERFUL just the way they are. Who but a three-year-old, proudly describing his achievements, could say, "I can put the bread in the toaster, but I can't flush it!"

Who but a pig-tailed six-year-old could cry, gazing at a pond ruffled by a breeze, "Look, Mommy, the lake's getting a permanent!"

Who but a worried nine-year-old, having heard a hurricane warning on the radio, could write this last will and testament: "I leave my bike and my dog and everything I own to my friend George Reynolds—if he isn't blown away first!"

Who but a curly-headed four-year-old could start off his evening prayers with such a beguiling question as: "Our Father, Who art in Heaven, how'dja know my name?"

When kids act or talk like this, parents can hardly be blamed for wishing that they'd never grow up. But they have to grow up, and it's the parents' job to help them. You can argue that it's the most important job in the world, this business of "bending the twig." And when it's done well, it's the most rewarding and satisfying thing in the world. So let's talk about it a little bit.

Small Chips and Old Blocks

THERE USED TO BE an old joke about the father who warned his son not to go to the burlesque show, because he'd see dreadful sights if he did. Naturally the kid sneaked off at the first opportunity and went to the show where—sure enough—he saw a dreadful sight: his dad!

There can be a lot of wisdom hidden in a joke, and I think there's a lot in this one. The kid who went to the burlesque show was literally following in his father's footsteps. His father's footsteps led in the wrong direction, and so. . . .

The moral is pretty obvious: when it comes to forming your child's character, the most important single factor is the example you set as a parent. You can discourage undesirable friends, you can forbid certain TV programs or movies, you can ban comic books or stock the kid's room with classics, you can send him to the best Sunday school in town, you can preach and exhort and threaten and point to the lives of famous men. . . .

But when it comes to character formation, none of these things will affect your child one tenth as much as his daily observations of *you.*

This is a scary thought, but there's no getting around it. Most kids are born emotionally intact. If they grow up badly warped, it's because their environment warped them. And in their early years, the formative years, their environment is pretty much what their parents make it.

There are whole libraries full of books on how to bend a twig, many by experts who devoted their whole lives to the subject. Lois and I read some of those books, and got a lot out of them, and I recommend the same procedure to you.

I don't intend these words of mine to be in any sense a substitute for the findings of the experts. But it's true that every married couple has to take these findings and try to apply them to the specific problems of their own kids. That's what Lois and I did, and in the process we developed a sort of blueprint of our own. It's this philosophy—pardon the fancy term—that I want to pass along to you as painlessly as possible in the pages of this book.

So, to begin with, here are six rules of thumb (a green thumb, I hope) on how to bend a twig.

1. *Take a Good Look at Yourself*

This first rule, of course, is based on the premise that kids consciously or unconsciously pattern themselves on their parents. So if you have certain personality traits that you don't want your children to inherit, the best way to safeguard the children is to make a constant effort to get rid of those qualities in yourself.

I had a friend who decided, when his son was ten or eleven, that it would be better for the kid if he didn't smoke. This was back in 1952, when the first medical findings on the long-range effect of smoking on health began to appear. (I'll have more to say about this in the chapter on teen-agers.) My friend was a fairly heavy smoker. He knew that if he just decided to quit for his own good, he wouldn't have the motivation or the determination to do it.

So he decided to take his son into his confidence. He told him that he was going to try gradually to quit smoking and made the kid a kind of monitor or supervisor in the deal. Every afternoon, when the father would come home from work, he'd make a report to his son. Some days he'd have a good effort to report; some days not so good. The youngster kept a log on the number of cigarettes his dad smoked. They even worked out a graph, showing how the number tended to increase with emotional strain or tension.

As time went by, they grew so fascinated that their conference became the high point of the day for each of them. The first time the father was able to report a completely cigaretteless day, Junior broke open his piggy bank and bought two tickets to the Sunday ball game. Dad was so entranced with himself and his new-found companionship with his son that he finally quit

smoking altogether. And, needless to say, Junior doesn't smoke today.

In other words, one of the most effective keys to child-control is self-control. Make yourself the most effective person you possibly can. That's the best way to prevent in your children the handicaps that you deplore in yourself.

2. *Be Relaxed*

THE SECOND RULE for bending twigs is easy for some people and hard for others. It's important, though, because children are very sensitive to tension. A famous psychiatrist told me once that very small infants could tell with astonishing accuracy how their mother was feeling by the way she held them. If she was full of love and happiness, the child could sense it. If she was upset or angry or insecure, the baby knew it. The secret, the psychiatrist said, lay in the muscle-tensions of the mother. If she was relaxed, the child could feel the ease and assurance, and would respond to it. If she was not, the tension communicated itself through the muscles of her arms and body.

This sort of communication isn't limited to humans. If you're riding a horse, and become frightened, the horse knows it. And it makes *him* nervous. Same thing with kids: if you're ill at ease with them, they know it, and become uneasy themselves.

Most parents, after producing one or two children, lose their fear that maybe they're not handling the kid exactly right. This is a good thing, and another argument in favor of large families. Ask any parent of many: he'll tell you that the more kids you have, the better adjusted they seem to be, and the easier they are to handle. Why? Because the parent gets more and more relaxed in his dealings with them.

People who have few contacts with children are apt to betray their lack of confidence by over-effusiveness. We've all seen the well-meaning maiden aunt who pounces on little Charles with oohs and ahs that conceal a world of inexperience. We've also seen little Charles' grim reaction to this approach.

Recently, in a letter, one of my televiewers told me about a female friend of the family who appeared in her house after a lapse of several years, took one look at the son and heir, and gushed, "Why, Johnny, the last time I saw you, you were only THIS high!" To which Johnny replied, "Yes, and the last time I saw you, you were only THIS wide!"

Another little girl I knew, on being saluted with the usual: "Goodness, Martha, you've grown another foot!" looked down at her shoes. "Really?" she said coolly, "I only see two." I don't know yet whether she was being innocent or devastating!

It's not always easy to be relaxed with kids. Fathers, I think, have it easier than mothers, who are constantly on the firing line. Another friend of mine reported this brief and poignant dialogue between her five-year-old and seven-year-old the other day:

"I'm bored. Let's do something."

"What'll we do?"

"Let's play drive-Mummy-crazy!"

"Oh, goodie! Let's!"

At certain stages of their career, kids seem to have just one purpose in life: to reduce their parents to gibbering neurotics. One member of our tribe—I won't mention names—went through a phase of ultra-exactitude. If you said it was ten o'clock, she pointed out that it was actually nine fifty-nine and a half. If you said the sun was shining, she would gaze earnestly around until she found a small cloud, and remind you gently that it wasn't shining under *that*. This was hard to deal with, because, technically, she was always right. We finally came up with a cure. Every time she did it, the victim was allowed to point a silent and accusing finger at her, and say nothing at all. In fact, *everybody* was allowed to point an accusing finger. She soon got over it!

I think the best remedy for the mother who really feels the screaming meemies closing in on her is simply to get away for a little while. Call in Grandma, hire a sitter, or even invent a deep freeze where you could stow 'em for a week or so and then take 'em out as good as new. Park them temporarily with friends, do anything, but get away, go to a movie, have your hair done, buy a new hat.

Then, when you come back, you'll be a much happier person, and a much better parent. Why? Because you'll be following Rule Number Two: you'll be relaxed.

3. *Assert Your Authority*

In any organization, discipline is essential, and to enforce discipline there must be authority— and respect for authority. This is equally true of an army, a business corporation, or a family. The less authority, the more confusion. When authority breaks down completely, the door is wide open to chaos.

A lot of European and Asiatic parents think that in this department of child raising we Americans have dropped the ball completely. A couple of years ago, an Oriental visitor was asked what impressed him most about the United States. "I think," he said politely, "it's the way parents obey their children."

To some extent, I think the child psychologists of two or three decades ago are responsible for this. When their studies and researches with disturbed children indicated that parental harshness or too severe discipline was often to blame, they made the very human mistake of going to the opposite extreme. They preached that, since acute frustration obviously was bad for kids, then total "self-expression" must be the answer.

They had some pretty persuasive spokesmen, too. As a result, the great American public, just becoming aware of the new science of psychiatry, was completely taken in. Every tantrum, every piece of childish mischief was regarded as evidence that the kid had been frustrated, or not loved enough. Instead of resorting to the instinctive and useful smack on the bottom, the parent went into an agitated huddle with himself, often emerging with a galloping guilt complex and the shuddery conviction that if he deprived Junior of a single lollipop, Junior would inevitably wind up as a mass murderer.

The result was a whole generation of parents who were actually terrified of their own children—and a whole generation of children who were spoiled, obnoxious, bewildered brats. I'm no sociologist, but it wouldn't surprise me if there was a definite connection between the push-over parents of the 1930's and 40's and the rise of juvenile delinquency that has plagued us so bitterly in the 1950's.

The pendulum is swinging rapidly, now. Fathers are being urged to re-establish themselves as the head of the household. Mothers are being advised to give orders and make them stick. But you can't reverse a trend like this overnight. In too many American families, fathers still tend to be voiceless and unconsulted drudges, and mothers still regard themselves as a kind of harassed and unpaid servant whose function it is to pick up clothes, anxiously ascertain food preferences and provide same, stand by for twenty-four-hour chauffeur service, and so on.

From the beginning, in our family, Lois and I tried to make it clear to the kids that while we loved them and would make any reasonable sacrifice for them, they were *not* rulers of the roost, or anything approaching it. They were first dependents, and later junior partners in the family corporation. As such, they had limited privileges and definite obligations. The obligations included obedience to family rules, and deference to the wishes of the senior partners—Lois and myself.

Sure, we've had disobediences and minor mutinies. It

would be a spineless sort of kid who didn't rebel once in a while. But those infractions carried with them penalties of one kind or another, and the kids had sense enough, most of the time, to realize that the discomfort or deprivation of the penalties outweighed the pleasure of the infractions.

I once heard a wise woman say that, in her opinion, selfish parents made the best parents. This startled me at the time, but I think I know now what she meant. She meant that parents who put the convenience and casual pleasure of their children ahead of their own convenience or desires are making a big mistake. They are abdicating authority, and in so doing they are damaging both the kids and themselves.

At the other extreme from parents who slavishly try to do everything for their kids are those who have no authority because they do nothing. We tend to think that this sort of parent exists mainly in the lower income groups, and statistically this may be true. But there are plenty of well-heeled parents who don't give a darn either.

Sometimes they hand kids over to servants and forget them. Sometimes they seem to think schools or camps can take a parent's place. Sometimes, weirdly enough, they get so involved in civic affairs and do-gooding activities designed to enhance their social status or sense of importance that they neglect their own kids.

I remember one night when Jack and Lois and I were

driving home late and passed a couple of kids we knew
—boys in their early teens. They were standing under
a street light, and they watched our car carefully and
furtively, as if they were afraid we might be cops. I
said something disapproving about kids being on the
streets at that time of night, and Lois agreed. "There's
nothing for them to do but get into trouble," she said.
"Why aren't they home where they belong?"

Jack said, "Maybe because nobody cares where they
are or what they do."

There it was in a nutshell: no authority because nobody cared.

That's why our Rule Number Three for parents who
want to bend twigs successfully is: *Assert Your Authority.* Assert it, and make it stick!

4. *Don't Expect Miracles*

THIS RULE IS a pretty good one to apply
in all your dealings with people, but we have found it
particularly important in trying to cope with kids. I
am not the most patient person in the world with myself, and there are times, I am sure, when I expect too
much of others.

With kids, this is both unfair and unwise. Unfair because very often they simply haven't reached that level

of achievement yet. And unwise because if you constantly demand more than a child can give, you damage his confidence and may even end by making him doubt his value as a human being.

As I indicated in the last chapter, Lois and I made the mistake of thinking that all our kids would be like Jack, who was always a mature, stable, well-balanced child. But they *weren't* all like Jack. Sharon was also born wise beyond her years. But Dawn and Robert developed much more slowly, and Diane has much more emotional range than either Jack or Sharon.

Jack was a natural competitor; he would loaf along until the going got tough, then he would make a sudden effort. His school work reflected this: he was just so-so in day-to-day grades. But when an exam or a test came along, he'd fly at it and do very well. Dawn was just the opposite. When a big test would come along, she'd study hard, she'd know it all, and then at the critical moment, her mind would go blank—or almost blank— and she'd do poorly. And I'm quite sure that one cause of her nervousness was her feeling that we, her parents, expected from her the same kind of performance that we'd had from Jack.

The truth is, it's hard for a parent to remember how big and menacing the world looks when you're a child. "Come on," we say a bit impatiently when our four-year-old falls down and skins her knees. "Be a big, brave girl!" But she's not a big, brave girl. She's a small one who's been hurt and is frightened. She wants and needs our love and sympathy, not a lecture on courage.

I remember the time, a few years back, when a pre-dawn earthquake hit Los Angeles. The house shook like a wet terrier, waking everyone out of a sound sleep to the eerie feeling of topsy-turvydom. Joints were squealing as the two-story house swayed back and forth. Dishes and bric-a-brac rattled on shelves. And strange, unidentifiable sounds gave one a chilled, apprehensive feeling.

As quickly as it started, it was over, and all was quiet for two seconds. Then Lois and I heard the slam of bedroom doors, the patter of bare feet, and the sobs of fright as five little Links streamed out of their rooms and landed in our big bed. In an instinctive reaction to unspeakable terror, they just came running. It was the biggest traffic jam any bed has survived, and the tangled mass of humanity was mute testimony to the way fear can trigger human emotion.

Our own fright was forgotten in our efforts to reassure the youngsters. I learned then and there, and I've often thought since, that the best antidote for any fear is the demand of others on your own courage and steadfastness. If there had been no children in the house, we'd have been paralyzed.

Modern children, especially, fool you because they grow up physically and mentally so fast. They acquire astounding vocabularies by the time they're five, often just by listening to television programs. But their rate of *emotional* growth is the same as it always was. The result of all this is that very often parents misjudge youngsters and tend to treat them as pint-sized adults instead of kids.

Sometimes, I think, this tendency goes right up into the teens. Modern teen-agers certainly do their best to convince you that they're grown up, with high heels and lipstick at thirteen, and cigarettes at fourteen, and so on. But they're not really mature. Behind the façade they erect so carefully are all sorts of uncertainties and insecurities and mute appeals for help. They're confused themselves, because part of them wants to stay in the nest and another stronger part is urging them to become independent. But they are by no means as self-sufficient as they pretend to be, or would like to be, and it's a mistake to think they are.

So don't expect miracles from kids—at any age. You won't get them. And one of the surest roads to unhappiness and dissatisfaction is to go around expecting something that you can never get.

5. *Don't Change Signals in Mid-Stream*

A CERTAIN AMOUNT of consistency is advisable in almost anything, from your golf swing to brushing your teeth. In dealing with kids, it's important too—because few things upset a child more than indecisive or erratic treatment from the two people who represent law and order and stability in his world—his parents.

I remember once meeting a man who had recently acquired a puppy. It was a retriever, a well-bred, intelligent animal. The man had been "training" him for a week or so, and his idea of training was to pet the dog one minute and shout harshly at him the next. The dog was a nervous wreck. The man was disgusted with the animal: no hunting instinct, he said. The truth was, he had the poor thing so confused and frightened and resentful that any retrieving instinct it might have had was completely paralyzed.

Kids are a lot more sensitive than dogs. One of the most sullen and unattractive teen-agers I know is a Junior Miss whose mother is what you might call a disciplinary weather-vane. One week she'll decide the kid is too young for lipstick, so the rule is laid down: no lipstick. Positively none. Then, at her bridge club, she'll discover that two other mothers allow lipstick on their offspring of similar age. So the ban is off. Then Grandma comes to the house, takes one look, disapproves loudly, and—presto! The ban is on again. It's a routine that would drive a sphinx to nervous prostration, let alone a youngster trying to navigate the rapids between adolescence and womanhood.

Sometimes the consequences can be really serious. I knew of an actor here in Hollywood, a temperamental and high-priced star, who had a son of about sixteen, the child of one of his earlier marriages. The boy lived with his father, who treated him either with great severity or with lavish generosity, depending on how he was feeling. In one of his mellow moods, he gave the kid an expensive sports car.

So what happens? So one fine night the kid goes out and *steals* a car, although his own car was sitting right in front of the house. He drives it at eighty miles per hour until a cop catches up with him. Naturally, he lands in jail.

Why? A psychiatrist familiar with the case told me that there were half a dozen reasons. But the main one was that the kid was sick and tired of unpredictability. He wanted to show the world, and his father in particular, that he could be unpredictable too. If he hurt his old man in the process, why, so much the better. It was one way of expressing the resentment he was feeling.

In that case, I think it might have been better if the father had been severe all the time, or indulgent all the time. The kid probably could have adjusted to either kind of treatment. But he couldn't stand the violent swings from one extreme to the other.

I think parents must try to achieve consistency not only as individuals but as a team. If Dad is tough and Mother is trying to compensate by being soft, if Mother issues an order and Father countermands it, the same sort of jittery environment is created.

It's no environment to grow up in. Watch it—for your kids' sake, and your own.

6. *The Balance Wheel of Love*

THE LAST RULE, and by far the most important is: *give your kid the right amount of love.* This isn't as easy as it sounds. Almost every parent will tell you without hesitation that he loves his child. But "love" is a big word, and a slippery one. And it means different things to different people.

We've all seen cases where a possessive and domineering mother just about ruins a child's life. The mother thinks she is motivated by love. Actually, it is "smother"

love . . . a neurotic outlet for the frustrations and bitternesses boiling inside Mama.

We've all known parents who ignore their kids most of the time and then try to make up for such neglect with an expensive present, beautifully wrapped, with a card enclosed saying: "Much love from Dad." But such a gift doesn't really represent love; it's often just a sop to the parent's guilty conscience.

It's a tricky business, and no two cases are alike. Some kids need more reassurance than others; these are the ones who need warm, demonstrated affection. Others are more independent; they are likely to resent too much demonstrativeness on the part of their parents. It makes them feel trapped.

Each child's needs are different, but I think it's safe to say that, right from the start, every kid needs to feel that there is someone strong and loving and protective standing behind him, ready to help him out of any jam he may get in, willing to love him no matter what happens. Psychiatrists say that we never lose this need, that it goes right through life with us. Many people, when they become adult, find this sort of reassurance and support in a devout religious faith.

Certainly tiny babies need love and protection. A friend of mine who worked as a volunteer in a big hospital told me once about an infant of three months that kept having convulsions. The doctors could find nothing physically wrong. But they learned that the mother hadn't wanted the child, would never pick it up or cuddle it, just propped a bottle in the crib when feeding time came. When the nurses in the hospital began giving the child some normal affection, the convulsions stopped. They were a protest, the most violent one the kid could make, against being deprived of love.

Such a mother, fortunately, is most unusual. In most parents the love-instinct is so strong that the main danger is that it will lead to over-indulgence and spoiling. A lady stopped me on the street not long ago and asked if I thought it was possible to spoil very small babies. I said, yes, I thought it was possible to spoil people at any age. If a tiny baby learns that every time he yelps you will pick him up, he's going to blackmail you day and night. If a three-year-old finds that a tantrum gets him his own way, he'll specialize in tantrums.

Even grown-ups can be spoiled if attention and flattery and the luxuries of life come too easily. We movie and television stars have to be particularly careful about this. People defer to us, admire us, go out of their way to make things easy for us. Now and then I find myself getting quite snappish because—let's say— I can't get reservations instantly on a jet plane to New York, or six seats to the best musical in town. "Watch it, Linkletter," I always say to myself. "Your hat-band seems to be shrinking!"

I suppose it's harder to spoil a very small child than a larger one. An African explorer told me once that the pygmies over there have a pretty good system. They spoil and pet and coddle a new baby—until the next one comes along. Then *he* gets the gold-plated treatment, and his predecessor just becomes one more member of the tribe. Works fine, my friend said; he never saw a single neurotic pygmy. Or else their neuroses were so small that he just couldn't see them!

I think you can tell when a kid is getting roughly the amount of love he needs by the way he acts. If he's generally happy, enthusiastic, out-going, he's probably all right. Another good indication is how much affection he gives back to the world in general—or to you. If he likes to sit in your lap, runs to meet you when you come home, flings his arms around your neck at bedtime, chances are you don't have much to worry about.

I've always liked the story one of my televiewers sent in. Her little daughter, aged three, looked up at her one day with adoring eyes. "Mummy," she said, "when I grow up, I'm going to get you an electric stove, and an electric iron—and an electric chair!"

It was a momentary "shock" for Mummy, but there was no mistaking the sentiment behind the promise. It was pure reflected love . . . the most heart-warming thing in the world.

Chapter 3

Slightly Fallen Angels

KIDS ARE IRRESISTIBLE when they offer you a combination of shrewdness and innocence that no adult could possibly match. The other day on our House Party program I asked a young lady of about five what her mother did for fun.

"She plays golf," she said, "With a strange man."

"A strange man?" I echoed. "Don't you know who he is?"

She shook her head. "Nobody knows who he is," she said darkly.

I thought I had better change the subject. "Any other news?" I asked briskly.

"Well," she said, "Mama's going to have a baby, but no one knows why."

Whereupon, with shrieks of delight, the studio audience fell into the aisles, and somewhere a perfectly respectable housewife—who no doubt had been taking some innocent lessons from a golf pro—wished she could climb into a divot and pull the turf over her head.

Once bitten, twice bitten. A few days later I tried the same question on a young man of seven. "What does your dad do for fun?" I asked him, while millions watched and listened.

"Well," he said a bit sadly, "he used to like hunting and fishing, but now he's just interested in indoor sports."

"What sort of indoor sports?" I inquired.

"I don't know," he said. "He always shuts the door."

A giggle from the audience warned me not to pursue this line of inquiry. "What does your mother do for fun?" I queried.

"I don't know for sure," he said doubtfully. Then his face brightened. "But I know she bought a nightie to go on a vacation!"

And the audience exploded again.

This question, "What do your parents do for fun?",

of course, is a gimmick designed to unlock family secrets, and the more unexpected the revelation, the more delighted the audience reaction. One youngster, I remember, confided that his father was a psychiatrist.

"And what does he do for fun?" I asked, braced for anything.

"He reads comics in the bathtub," was the serene reply.

Another kid revealed that his mother's idea of fun was playing football after Sunday School.

"What position?" I asked.

"Stooped over in front of the church!" he said proudly.

But for sheer volume of laughs, you can't beat the slightly ribald statement delivered with an air of poker-faced innocence. One more, and then I'll move on to more serious things. I asked this young man, aged about six, what his daddy did for fun.

"He sleeps out on the porch," he said.

"Why is that?" I wanted to know.

"Because Mama keeps thrashing around in bed all night and he can't have any fun there at all!"

Halos—Lost, Strayed or Stolen

KIDS ARE SO MUCH FUN most of the time that we harassed parents are ready to forgive them almost anything. Which is just as well, because sometimes there's quite a lot to forgive. Being human, kids have their faults. And since their powers of self-control are not fully developed, the faults can be pretty glaring, at times.

A wise old doctor told me once that the secret of discipline, where kids are concerned, is to remember that a child never does *anything* unless he is getting some kind of satisfaction out of it. And the more I've watched kids, the truer the statement seems.

A three-year-old, for example, who starts to belabor his baby sister with the nearest available piece of lumber isn't doing it just for kicks. He sees, in the unwelcome creature in the crib, a real threat to his own position in the family, a possible rival for his mother's affection. So he wants to get rid of it.

A nervous youngster like our Robert, who gets a sick tummy at school, doesn't enjoy being nauseated. But if his symptoms result in his prompt removal from a situation that he doesn't like (school) by a person whose sympathetic attention he wants very much (Mother or Dad), then the momentary unpleasantness of being sick is worth it.

What I'm trying to say is that kids are not born "bad," and they're not likely to act "badly" unless they're getting something out of it. If the parent can figure out what that something is, and supply it in some other way, then the "badness" is quite likely to disappear.

When parents complain about kids' behavior, it seems to me that the gripes and laments could almost be classified into half a dozen categories. There are thousands of specific crimes and misdemeanors and behavior lapses, but most of them are traceable to what might be called the Six Ugly Attitudes. These Ugly Six crop up in kids everywhere, to the detriment of law and order and the dismay of parents. So let's take the six and see if we can figure out what lies behind each one. Most behavior faults in kids are just symptoms of more basic causes. And the more you know about the causes, the easier it is to deal with the symptoms.

1. *The Green-Eyed Monster*

A PSYCHIATRIST WHOSE OPINION I value once told me that in large families, or even small ones, when the kids quarrel and fight among themselves, at least half the time what they are really fighting over is their parents' love. I don't know whether this is literally true (psychiatrists have a way of making statements that you can't disprove), but there's no doubt that jealousy does play a large part in many small lives.

We have some friends with five children, four girls and a boy. Right now Girl Number Two is going through a phase where she obviously dislikes Girl Number Four. She can't express this dislike too openly— her parents jump on her if she does. So she needles Girl Number Four in all sorts of sly and ingenious ways. If Number Four draws a picture or builds a sand-castle or dresses her doll in different clothes, Number Two will mutter something derogatory. If Girl Number Three suggests a game, Girl Number Two will at once do her best to exclude Girl Number Four. And so it goes.

Girl Number Two isn't basically mean or sadistic, but quite obviously something in her has decided that she isn't getting her fair share of parental attention and affection. Possibly the real target of her resentment is Baby Brother, and she disguises it by picking on Girl Number Four. In any case, her behavior sets up a vicious circle, because her parents become exasperated with her and scold her, which naturally makes her feel more unloved than ever, and more resentful.

It takes a lot of insight and understanding on the part of the parents to deal with a situation like this, and it's a situation that exists in literally millions of families. In most cases, no doubt, the jealous child outgrows his jealousy, or finds a not-too-damaging outlet for his fear and anger. But sometimes, if the parents play favorites too obviously, the child who feels neglected can have his personality permanently warped.

I knew a family once where there were two children, boy and girl. The boy, who was a couple of years older, had rheumatic fever, and wound up with a damaged heart. The parents knocked themselves out trying to make up to the kid for the blow life had dealt him. Nothing was too good for Junior; every whim had to be gratified. His sister had to pick up whatever crumbs she could find.

This was bad enough for Junior, but the effect on the younger child was shattering. She was a pretty girl, and eventually married quite a nice man. But she was always convinced that she was getting the short end of every stick, the raw end of every deal. Nothing was ever enough for her; her ego was so starved that no amount of attention could satisfy it. Her husband gave up, finally, and got a divorce. Last I heard, she was still staggering through life, a pathetic and ruined figure whose endless refrain is: "What about me?"

No doubt this was an extreme example of childhood jealousy or "sibling rivalry"—a phrase I detest because it makes me think of slimy things under a microscope, not the honest problems of growing kids. I mention it only to remind parents of the importance of sharing their love equally among all their children. Or, if they don't love them equally, at least they should pretend that they do!

If you're the parent of more than one child, you might as well face the fact that there's going to be an occasional visitation from the green-eyed monster. Kids are born selfish; they have to learn to share things. The more precious the thing is, the harder it is to share it, and nothing is more precious to a child than Mother's or Dad's love.

So be prepared for the fights and quarrels that are an expression of this rivalry. And remember: the more fairly you divide yourself among your kids, the less fighting there will be.

2. *Man or Mouse?*

JEALOUSY IS ONE COMMON personality de-
fect in kids; timidity is another. I'd say that it's more
likely to occur in girls than in boys, but boys are by no
means immune. And excessive timidity in kids worries
the daylights out of parents, because they know that to
get along in life a person has to have a certain amount
of drive and confidence—and timidity robs its victims
of both.

I've heard it said that newborn babies have only two
fears: fear of falling, and fear of loud noises. Maybe
so, but some kids add to their collection fast. Without
any coaching at all, they can work themselves into a
dither over such diverse things as thunder, the dark,
dogs, fire-engines, vacuum cleaners, elevators, or even
the thought of dying.

When you stop to think about it, a lot of these fears
are perfectly understandable. How does a one-year-old
know that the roar of a vacuum cleaner isn't a threat
directed right at him? Or take fear of the dark, for
instance. What adult hasn't felt his hackles rise when
reading a ghost story alone at midnight? What woman
likes to be alone in a house after dark? All you need to
do is combine imagination and the unknown to scare
yourself into quite a tizzy, even when you know it's
silly. So why shouldn't a small child do the same?

Then there are bad dreams. Nightmares can be terri-

fying when you're fifty, let alone five. I always sympa-
thized with the youngster who tapped at midnight on
her parents' door. "Mommy," she said, "can I come
into your room? My room doesn't have very good
dreams!"

All kids, I think, are afraid of *something*, so a reasonable amount of timidity is normal enough. But some
kids are more fearful than others. These tend to be
high-strung, imaginative children. They observe certain facts, then jump to all sorts of dreadful conclu-
sions. Like the five-year-old one of my viewers told me
about who had a new baby sister. The grandmother was
helping out while the mother rested, and decided to

give the baby a bath. She undressed the baby on the kitchen table, then lit and opened the oven to warm the room. Whereupon the five-year-old rushed to his' mother in a panic. "Mommy, Mommy!" he yelled. "Grandma's getting the baby ready to bake it!" Right observation; wrong conclusion!

If a kid has the kind of imagination that populates the dark with witches, dragons, or black widow spiders, you may have to insulate him to some extent. Cut down on excitement at bedtime. Avoid scary stories or horror movies like the plague. Never threaten him with bogeymen (or policemen, for that matter—my friend Alfred Hitchcock is still scared to death of cops because his father once jokingly had him locked in a cell when he was a kid). Don't belittle the child's fears or expect him to conquer them all at once. If he wants his bedroom door left open a crack, or a small nightlight in his room, let him have these little aids to reassurance. If his fears are really abnormal, or seem to be increasing, don't fool around—consult your doctor.

Somtimes timidity hangs on for quite a while. It did with our Dawn, and to some extent with Robert. I'll never forget the time we decided to send Dawn to summer camp. We figured it would do her good to get out from under our sheltering wings. She was nine or ten at the time.

Well, sir, she came back the dirtiest girl ever seen on land or sea. She had impetigo, athlete's foot—everything but fleas. We couldn't understand how she got so dirty in a place where daily showers were required. We finally found out that she was afraid of the shower-room because it was rather dark and the pipes gurgled at her—so she'd been faking her showers! She'd go in, and hide just behind the door. So, for practically two months, she'd had no baths. It took innumerable bars of soap and several medical treatments to restore her to normalcy.

As I said in an earlier chapter, Dawn finally outgrew her timidity completely. Most kids do, if they get a steady flow of affection and encouragement from the people who mean most to them—Mom and Dad.

So if you've got a shrinking violet on your hands, don't be too discouraged. Put him or her in situations where you know the child will do well. Don't force him to face his fears; build up his confidence by giving him things to do that he likes to do and can do well. That way you'll create a "climate of success." And as confidence grows, fear will diminish.

3. *The Holy Terrors*

THE OPPOSITE OF TIMIDITY or shyness is over-aggressiveness. Here the culprits are usually boys. Some of 'em seem to be born with a built-in surplus of destructiveness, vandalism, hostility, and pig-headedness. They act as if the world was a nail and they were a hammer. They're going to hammer that nail clear out of sight, no matter how many sparks fly or thumbs get mashed in the process.

"What's the main trouble around your house?" I asked a seven-year-old on our House Party program the other day.

"All the fights between brothers and sisters," he replied promptly.

"Can't you figure out a way to stop them?" I asked.

"No," he said. "But I know how to START them!"

Another youngster on that same program had a band-aid on his leg. "Where'd you get that scratch?" I asked him.

"My brother pushed me over a wall."

"And what did you learn from that experience?"

"To run faster," he said sadly.

Every large family is likely to have at least one of these small demons who seems, at times, to be a cross between a tornado and Attila the Hun. Dealing with them is tough, because ordinary punishments bounce off like hail on a tin roof. Here's a vivid scene of family life depicted in four lines of unrehearsed dialogue between myself and a young lady of six:

"What's the funniest thing you've ever seen?"

"My mother chasing a pest with a fly-swatter."

"What pest?"

"My brother!"

I think we'd all agree that a certain amount of exuberance in kids is fine. Psychiatrists say that we're all

born with, or soon develop, these feelings of aggression
—and that eventually most of us turn them into useful
channels: athletic competition, fighting to make a living, struggling to eliminate evil and injustice from the
world, and so on. Very often, I think, your obstreperous
kid is merely demonstrating the fact that he's got his
full share of these impulses, but hasn't yet developed
the necessary controls. He's all horsepower and no
brakes. This is hard on the furniture, and on Mother's
nerves, but it's nothing to be alarmed about. In fact,
it's probably something to be thankful for.

But now and then you see kids whose destructive impulses and outbursts of hostility are clearly manifestations of something other than the normal amount of
healthy aggressiveness. In teen-agers, this can become
delinquency. In smaller children, I think, it's often a
protest of some kind, a declaration—however senseless
and stupid it may seem—that something is wrong. The
kid isn't getting or *feels* that he isn't getting something
that he needs: love, security, admiration, affection,
something.

The borderline between normal aggressiveness and
abnormal psychology is a shadowy one, and I'm not
qualified to point it out. In fact, I think it's dangerous
to generalize too much: all cases are different, and some
of them are very complicated.

So all I will say is this: if you have a "holy terror" in
your home, and you feel that his rambunctiousness is
just plain vitality and high spirits running a little bit

wild, don't worry about it. Try to guide it and control it, but don't try to kill it (you'd be breaking the main-spring that some day may drive the kid triumphantly through life). Grit your teeth, patch up the holes in the plaster, put band-aids on the other kids, and double your liability insurance. He'll grow out of it.

On the other hand, if you have a kid who seems habit-ually withdrawn and sullen, who seems to hate the world in general and you in particular, who expresses his hatred in actions ranging from petty spite to major sabotage, then you ought to get help from your family doctor, or a Child Guidance Clinic, or some qualified professional source.

Holy terrors are probably okay. Unholy terrors are emotionally sick. Try to keep the difference in mind.

4. *I, Me, My, Mine. . . .*

QUITE OFTEN parents admit to me, in a rather shamefaced way, that they are worried about their kids because they seem so self-centered. Never think of anyone but themselves. Have no sense of re-sponsibility. Won't share things, and so on. . . .

I think the most sensible view to take of Ugly Atti-tude Number Four, which is nothing in the world but plain, old-fashioned selfishness, is to face the fact that a certain amount of it is inevitable in kids—and in grownups too. Only the saints get rid of it all, and not many of us are saints. A newborn baby, obviously, is totally self-centered, and a toddler isn't much better. Kids only start to modify this self-centeredness when it begins to dawn on them that at times it turns their parents' love and approval into anger and disapproval —a state of affairs that they don't enjoy at all.

Most of us want to be liked and admired, and this includes kids. So when a child fails to grow out of his self-centeredness at a normal rate, it probably means one of two things. Either the kid isn't very bright, and can't gauge the effects of selfish behavior on other people or else something is wrong in his relationship to the people around him.

Sometimes it takes a kid fourteen or fifteen years to find out that selfishness really doesn't pay. I've seen spoiled, arrogant teen-agers do a complete back flip out of the rough of selfishness and onto the fairway of civilized behavior because they discovered, abruptly and painfully, that the girl or boy to whom they had taken a fancy didn't like them the way they were—and didn't hesitate to say so. Their parents had been pointing out their faults for years, but some kids get absolutely tone deaf where parental criticism is concerned. Sometimes it takes a disgusted glance from a friend, or a snip crack from the blonde down the street to make them take a new look at themselves.

I think selfishness is often prolonged in kids by parents who tend to make slaves of themselves for the kids' benefit. All this does is breed contempt for adults in general and parents in particular. The mother who meekly chauffeurs her daughter everywhere, the dad who **gives** Junior everything "because I had it tough when I was a kid and I want my children to have some fun," these parents aren't leading their youngsters away from their in-born selfishness—they're perpetuating it. And it's really unfair to the kids, because life is not going to treat them with kid gloves later on.

So where this problem of self-centeredness is concerned, remember that your child is born selfish and will need the best part of a lifetime to get over it. Don't expect too much too soon, but try to set a good example by being unselfish yourself. Help the kid see that popularity and success in life seldom come to totally self-centered people. Teach him the difficult art of sharing —by sharing yourself with him.

5. *"Some of My Best Small Friends Are Crooks"*

NOT LONG AGO a mother I know came across a fifty cent piece in her eight-year-old daughter's school-bag. She was aghast because she always gave the child a quarter for lunch—no more and no less. A little cross-examination confirmed her fears. The youngster had taken the money from a fellow-student's desk.

The mother rushed to the school principal, literally in tears. He listened to her with quiet sympathy and offered her his handkerchief. "Mrs. Jones," he said, "I don't blame you for being upset. We've all been taught that stealing is a serious crime, and it frightens a parent to see evidence of it in her child. But let me tell you a secret. Some of my best small friends are crooks!"

He went on to tell her that this sort of petty pilfering was very common in children around seven, eight, or nine, even when they had a reasonable number of toys and possessions, or had an allowance of their own. "It seldom becomes a habit," he said. "It's more likely to be one or two isolated episodes, like this one. It isn't a premeditated thing. The child just does it on impulse."

"But why?" cried the bewildered Mrs. Jones.

"I can't tell you exactly," the principal said. "But I can make a few guesses. Maybe your daughter feels a little lonely at this stage of the game. Maybe she's not as popular with her classmates as she would like to be. Maybe she planned to use that money to buy candy for the other kids—that's where this "stolen" money often goes. Or maybe—did you ever stop to think of this?—she wants to be independent of you. Maybe she's tired of having to accept *your* quarter, day after day. Then there's the possibility that she's in a group where swiping things becomes the daring and accepted thing to do. There are such groups, you know."

"What can I do?" asked the anxious mother. "I can't ignore it, can I?"

"No," said the principal, "you can't ignore it. The money has to be returned. The child has to be made to see that taking it was wrong, and won't be tolerated. But I'd be careful not to make a big thing of it. If you do, you'll just make the child feel lonelier than ever."

"But what if it happens again?"

"I don't think it will," the principal said. "The fact that you are here, and are so upset, shows that you care a lot about your child. The habitual stealers are almost always the kids who are seriously deprived of love and security at home. Don't worry; your youngster isn't a criminal. She isn't even abnormal. Just give her all the support and affection you can. It'll work out all right."

This was good advice, and Mrs. Jones took it. And the principal was right: the problem did not re-occur.

To me, the moral of the story is this: when the Fifth Ugly Attitude (dishonesty) rears its ugly head in one of your kids, don't go into an emotional tailspin about it. If you jump on the kid with both feet, and fill him with shame and guilt, you certainly aren't solving the problem, or getting to the root of it. You may just be making it worse.

Try to remember that kids very often haven't had time to develop clear-cut standards of right and wrong. Even when they do know right from wrong, their powers of self-control are limited. A sudden, strong impulse can break down their moral defenses. So it isn't fair to judge them by adult standards.

There are times when I think parents expect more in the way of honesty from their kids than they do from themselves. Junior tells a lie, and gets in trouble. But does Dad stick strictly to the truth when telling his cronies at the club how he outsmarted seven competitors to land a certain big order, or how he told off the boss in grand style? Mary is in the family dog-house because she's suspected of cheating on a sixth-grade test. But what was Mother doing when she lied about Mary's age recently to enable her to ride half-fare on a train trip to visit Grandma?

And isn't it at least a bit confusing for kids when we glorify outlaws like Robin Hood or make movies about the life of Al Capone, and then preach at them about the importance of honesty and truthfulness and respect for law?

There are also times when I think there's a little larceny in all of us, from bank-robbers to sedate and cautious businessmen. One fellow I know, recognizing this impulse in himself, goes around stealing paper-clips from his friends' desks. Never more than one or two at a time, but he filches them with great stealth and cleverness. Makes him feel wonderfully depraved and daring, he says.

So let's not judge the kids too harshly. A trace of the Six Ugly Attitudes can be observed by almost any of us, any time we take the trouble to look. Where? In the mirror, that's where.

6. *Kids and Cruelty*

THE SIXTH UGLY ATTITUDE is one that is seldom discussed, but traces of it exist in almost every child, ranging from thoughtlessness through meanness to what seems like deliberate cruelty. And sometimes parents get pretty upset about it.

Very often, I think, what looks like cruelty or brutality in a child is nothing but lack of imagination. A two-year-old tugging enthusiastically on a cat's tail isn't trying to inflict pain: he simply wants to see if this interesting appendage is detachable or not. It never occurs to him that his experiment is hurting the cat, so he is really being less cruel than his daddy who catches a fish or shoots a quail for fun, or his mother who drops a live lobster into a pot of boiling water. Presumably they know what they're doing.

Kids are often said to be cruel when they exclude or ignore a child who is shy, or different. But here again it's doubtful if they are fully aware of the hurt they are inflicting. Many animals seemed to be governed by a herd instinct that makes them reject a newcomer or an outsider. I wouldn't be surprised if the same sort of instinct sometimes governs the behavior of children.

Grownups live in a world regulated by customs and manners designed to spare the feelings of those around them, but kids have to learn the rules painfully and slowly. I remember once, when Lois and I were out with one of our kids, we met a man who was terribly crippled. "Gosh," cried our pride and joy at the top of his lungs, "look at the crooked man!" We snatched him away, our faces burning a dull red, but he wasn't being consciously cruel. He just hadn't reached the age where he could put himself in the other fellow's shoes.

There's a stage kids go through that might be known as B.T.—before tact. One little girl I heard of looked up at her mother and said lovingly, "Mommy, you're so pretty. All but your face!" Another mother, fishing for a compliment perhaps, asked her six-year-old what he'd do if he came home from school one day and found her dying of a heart attack. "Gosh," said Junior with a stricken look, "I guess I'd have to fix my own lunch!"

Sometimes what sounds like callousness in kids is nothing but a kind of practicality. One little girl on our House Party program told me she had a brother and a sister, so I asked her which she liked best.

"My sister," she said unhesitatingly.

"And why is that?" I wanted to know.

"Because," she said happily, "she's always away at college!"

On the same program was a young man who announced that when he grew up he was going to be a veterinary and taxidermist. "If I can't cure 'em," he said cheerily, "I'll stuff 'em!" The S.P.C.A. might not wholly approve, but you must admit his plan had a certain logic!

Once in a while you'll find a kid who actually does seem to enjoy twisting a smaller kid's arm, tying tin cans to a dog's tail, throwing kittens into the well, or generally inflicting pain—which he knows very well to be pain—upon some animal or some other human being. Such a youngster needs help, psychiatric help, but you don't have to be a psychiatrist to see that very likely such cruelty is a form of displaced anger, resentment turned away from its real target and aimed at a target that can't strike back.

If a youngster is angry enough, and frustrated enough, he may attack society as a whole, and then we say he is a delinquent. And sometimes, when I read of another "quiet, mild-mannered, church-going" youngster who goes berserk and strangles his sweetheart, or kills a small child, I wonder if it isn't a violent and tragic backfire against all the rules and restrictions and regulations and prohibitions that made him so "quiet and well-mannered" for so many years.

The truth is, all of us have frustrations and disappointments in life, and all of us show flashes of anger and irritability at times. But most of us learn to control these impulses, or get rid of them in harmless ways like whacking a golf-ball or pulling weeds or beating somebody's ears off at handball or bridge.

So help your child find harmless channels for *his* pent-up emotions. When he's small, see that he has adequate room to play and toys that help him let off steam. When he's older, help him find friends and activities that keep him busy and interested. If he shows traces now and then of the Sixth Ugly Attitude, don't worry about it. Chances are good that he'll grow out of it.

Somebody once asked Archie Moore, the ageless Negro prize-fighter, how he overcame the juvenile delinquency that plagued him as a child.

"Simple," said Archie. "I grew up."

In Short . . .

IF YOU'RE AN AVERAGE PARENT, then, with an average set of kids, you'll undoubtedly have more than a nodding acquaintance with the Six Ugly Attitudes: jealousy, timidity, over-aggressiveness, selfishness, dishonesty, and callousness. There are probably half a dozen others that I haven't listed, but that's not the point. The point is that occasional manifestations of all these traits are inevitable in most kids, and are nothing to worry about so long as they don't become chronic or go to extremes.

Nobody can be on his best behavior all the time, and this includes kids. There will be times when the most good-natured youngster will be tired or hungry or cross, times when he's worried or harassed or afraid, times when the emotional tensions and pressures inside of him make him snarl or snap at somebody, usually the person nearest to him.

But does this make kids any different from grownups? I don't think so.

I remember a very human question a harassed mother put to me one day from our studio audience. "Why is it," she cried, "that my child behaves so much better when he's out visiting than he does at home?"

For once I was able to come up with a simple reply. "Madam," I said, "don't you?"

Chapter 4

Fun Can Be Big Business

HAVING WON MYSELF a weird reputation through such diverse activities as emceeing "People Are Funny," growing rice in Australia, sponsoring a modeling school, and marketing plastic bubbles to enlarge television screens, I'm not very surprised when every day's mail brings me glittering investment opportunities, ranging from Head-Shrinking Made Easy to Outer Space Subdivisions, Incorporated.

Most of them I manage to duck. But I'll never forget an enthusiastic young man named Reuben Klamer who burst into my office some time back waving a plastic hoop and a plan to produce millions of similar hoops.

My first reaction was to bar the doors, install camouflaged tiger traps at all entrances, electrify the fences, and hook up a direct telephone wire to the nearest booby hatch. But I made the mistake of talking to Mr. Klamer. "What would we do with millions of plastic hoops?" I wanted to know. "Kids gave up rolling hoops years ago when they stopped walking anywhere their parents could drive them or their bicycles could carry them."

"These aren't for rolling," he explained impatiently. "They're for orbiting around the hips. Like this!" He slipped the contraption over his head, gave a flip of the hip, and the darned thing began to revolve around his middle like a live snake.

Taking a firm grip on my checkbook, and a firmer one on my sanity, I invited Mr. K to get a head start before the men with the butterfly nets arrived. People are funny, all right, but this one was ridiculous.

One hour later the persuasive young gent had calmed my fears with the story of how this phenomenal hoop had started in Australia (made of reed and bamboo by Australian bushmen), had been sold by the million to kids Down Under, and was now in its first triumphant march across the United States, beginning right here in Los Angeles.

We jumped into my car, took a tour of the neighborhood, and sure enough . . . there were the kids out in the streets with red, green, or yellow hoops, dreamily staring into space while their hips gyrated wildly and their tummies put an Egyptian belly dancer's routine to shame.

One long look was enough for me; we jumped headlong into the craze. Linkletter Spin-a-Hoops were manufactured by twelve factories across the United States and became one of half a dozen varieties of the original "Hula Hoop," and within a few months about thirty million kids from two to seventy-two were looping, hooping and convoluting from coast to coast.

Like everything that becomes a craze, this fad produced some extravagant "champions" who claimed such feats as: (1) whirling the hoop ten thousand times before falling flat, throwing up or being brained by their parents; (2) looping twenty hoops at the same time from neck to knees, like whirling dervishes from the Arabian Nights; (3) making the hoop travel from the ankles to the neck like a yo-yo without losing a beat or peeling an Adam's apple; (4) walking, jumping, running, skipping and dancing while maintaining the undulating monster's steady rhythm.

And suddenly it was over. The tidal wave ebbed away in all directions until only a few remote puddles of plastic remained to remind dazed and unbelieving parents that it had really happened. In six short months, the biggest, most sensational, nuttiest craze in the history of toy business had come and gone, leaving in its wake such unheard of medical oddities as calloused hips, water on the thigh, spaghetti spine and a generation of unfulfilled "bump" artists.

It also, mercifully, left stranded jokes such as this one:

"What is a naval destroyer?"

"A hula hoop with a nail!"

And, finally, it left me with an urge to find out more about the four billion dollar a year toy business that caters to the whims and fancies of the most tyrannical set of customers in the history of consumers: the kids of the U.S.A.

"All Play and No Work Makes Jack"—
for Some People

TWO BILLION DOLLARS! Does that figure surprise, or even astound, you? That's two thousand million dollars each year ladled out by parents, fond relatives and arriving house guests to make some forty million U.S. kids jump with joy—for an hour or two.

Roughly, here's how the grand total breaks down into its major classifications: Twenty per cent for dolls, 18 per cent for wheeled toys of all kinds, 5 per cent for guns, 9 per cent for games, 5 per cent for trains. And of course there are many smaller divisions that make up the rest of this amazing, amusing and colorful business.

It's a deadly serious business, though. Behind the funny toys and gaily colored gadgets you find a group of intent students of the secret world of kids. Like unsmiling gag-writers wrinkling their brows over the punch-line of a joke, these toy experts are constantly and scientifically probing every urge and impulse of the small fry to discover some new way to amuse or instruct their clients. Psychologists, philosophers, educators and inventors squeeze their brains for new approaches to the age-old yelp for fun.

This is appropriate enough, because by this time every parent knows that toys play a big role in the development of a child. Kids who learn how to play happily, psychologists have found, aren't very likely to blow their stacks later, when they have to face the real problems of life. If a child is given the right toys at the right time, the experts say, it helps him to grow and develop in the right way.

What to Give . . . and When

THE BEST JUDGE of a present is almost always the kid himself. Like the seven-year-old who wrote a Christmas thank-you note to his grandmother: "Dear Grandma, thank you very much for the nice gloves. I like them very much. But what I like most of all is the little dachshund puppy that I didn't get from you or anybody else. . . ."

The truth is, many grown-ups buy toys that fascinate *them*, but which may not be so much fun for Suzie or Junior. Or they buy toys that are too advanced, and frustrate the youngster rather than teach or amuse him. Or they choose toys that are too young for him and bore him silly.

Last year, on a People Are Funny show, we gave the mother of a four-year-old a chance to win $8,000 by telling us in advance which costume her child would pick from among these three: a sparkling party-dress, a space-girl suit or a cow-girl outfit. Unhesitatingly, the mother indicated the space-girl suit. And just as unhesitatingly, the tiny guest walked over and grabbed the cow-girl outfit. Out the window went the $8,000, and into the minds of millions of mothers all over the country must have popped the thought: "I wonder if I know my *own* child's dearest wish?"

It's worth some thought and study, because toys are no longer just meaningless trinkets. They're tools for play, and as such, tools for learning. This should be the object behind their purchase. They shouldn't be bought because the parent likes them, or because they remind him of his childhood, or to impress other adults, or to bribe the youngster into good behavior.

They shouldn't all be bought at Christmas or birthday-time, either. Most kids in this happy land are swamped at Christmas; a wise parent will put some of the items away and bring them out one at a time as the weeks go by. The average kid of eight or under frequently progresses more mentally and physically in a week than the average adult does in a year. As he grows and changes, he needs new challenges, and new kinds of fun.

For the harassed parent who would like some kind of guidance about what to buy and when, I have assembled a partial list of toys and a chronological chart that should shed a small ray of light through the dark jungle of playthings. What it all boils down to is fitting the toy to the child's capabilities and interests:

Very Small Fry, age zero to one year. Most normal babies appear to hear very well from birth, so a rattle or a bell attracts their attention almost from the start. The baby's first motor control, though, is over his eyes, so bright objects which he can follow visually are indicated. By the time he's six months old, he's busy examining the world around him with eyes, ears, fingers and mouth. He'll chew anything up to and including the family cat. He wants things that he can bang, bite, drop, push, shake and hear. This is the first indication of why "Rock, Rattle and Roll" is such a basic, universal musical urge.

So give him soft stuffed animals, bright plastic rattles, floating toys, musical toys, always making sure that playthings are too large to be swallowed, and that they are free of sharp edges, with non-toxic finishes.

The second year. At this age the kid is the greatest

explorer since Columbus. He wants to investigate, pick up, drop, carry, put into something or take out of something every object he can budge. So give him a wheel-barrow to push, a toy truck to ride on, put-together trains or boats, nests of blocks, dolls to put into doll carriages (if he's a girl!), easy wooden or plastic puzzles, and so on.

From two to four. Now the kid turns into a dynamo of action. He's developing so fast, physically, socially, and mentally, that there's practically nothing he won't tackle. So the choice becomes almost limitless. It's a good idea to include toys at this point that have to be shared: a wading pool, a sand-box, a set of swings or a slide. Sharing is one of the great necessities of life—and one of the most difficult lessons to learn. It's never too soon to start.

This is the age when play-acting begins, imitations of adult life. So the kids love toy luggage, toy telephones, play furniture, dolls' houses, dolls of all varieties, books that can be read aloud, and so on.

From four to six. At last the little demon is really becoming a member of society, so his toys should reflect his growing interest in other children as well as his need for strenuous play. Gym equipment and trampolines, tricycles and the first roller skates, police, fireman, nurse and cowboy outfits, a tent to pitch in the back yard where plots can be hatched to rob a bank or hold up a stagecoach. A phonograph with records. A set of magnetic darts. It's a wonderful, carefree, joyous age . . . the limitations of babyhood are gone and the responsibilities of school haven't started. (There are times when I wish I was exactly five-and-a-half again myself!)

From six to eight. Now the kid is very busy adjusting to the new demands of school. In the free time he has left, he needs a lot of physical activity to make up for his confinement in the classroom. So this is the age for bikes and scooters, kites and jump-ropes, punching bags, swim-flippers, shuffle board and stilts. By now the youngster is probably showing some creative ability. Hand puppets, small weaving looms, hobby assembly kits, building sets, toy sewing machines, work-benches, tool-chests—all these are useful and welcome.

From eight to ten. During this stage the kid is acquiring more skill and coordination. Now is the time for sports equipment of all kinds, books, the first cameras, simple archery, ping-pong, perhaps a miniature golf set. Kids in this age bracket like games of almost any type. Budding scientists will welcome a microscope or telescope. Musical kids may take to a harmonica or some other instrument. And so it goes, right on up to the shadowy line that divides childhood from the not-so-secret world of grown-ups.

Of course, not every child will fit into these categories. Some will be ahead of their age group; others behind. And being human, a lot of kids will want whatever it is that they haven't got. One day on our House Party program I asked a six-year-old, "What's your favorite toy?" And he brightly replied, "Anything my big sister is playing with!"

If that happens in your family, ask "big sister" to

let him have the toy for a while, and he'll soon discover he can't really enjoy it.

Of course, in the process of finding this out, he'll break it. From that point, I cease giving advice. Mommy and Daddy—you're on your own!

Bang—You're Dead!

WHILE WE'RE ON this subject of toys, I must report that quite often parents worriedly ask me what it means if Johnny is forever playing with toy guns, battleships and bombers, or is constantly pretending to shoot, hang, scalp or dismember practically everyone in sight. "Don't you think," they add fearfully, "that some of these toys actually stimulate violence in children?"

My answer to that is, "No, I don't." I think such toys liberate the violence that's already in the kid, and as a rule they liberate it harmlessly. The psychologists say that Johnny is actually worried at times because he feels so much hostility toward the grownups who're always fencing him in with don'ts. Popping off with his cap pistol at an imaginary bad man, or hanging in fantasy the bandit who bushwhacked the sheriff, gives him a chance to unload some of his grievances.

I've known well-meaning parents who make it a rule never to buy a lead soldier or a toy cannon for fear their kid will grow up to be a militarist or a war-monger—or something. I think this is silly. If you forbid a kid to have a toy gun, he'll create one out of a crooked stick, or just use his pointed finger with appropriate sound effects.

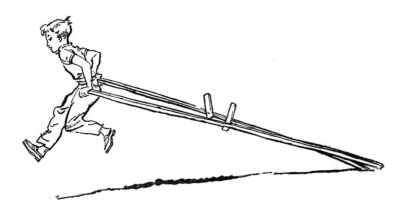

If we're honest about it, we'll admit that there is a lot of violence penned up in all of us. That's why football is so popular, why boxing has lasted all this time, why people seem to like those ridiculous wrestling matches. What's the most popular sport in the U.S.A. in terms of actual participation? It's bowling—a game where you joyously heave an object closely resembling a cannon-ball down a nice smooth straightaway and do your darndest to flatten ten wooden objects that can represent any target you choose—from your boss to your mother-in-law. And what do they call it when you knock them all down? A strike. Now, there's a lovely, lethal word. Strike! Makes you feel better just to say it.

So I say let Junior play soldier or sailor or space-man or cowboy, and let him arm himself with any imaginary weapon from battle-ax to death-ray pistol. All he can do with them is blow off steam, and it's better to have the steam outside of him than in.

There's a point, of course, where toy weapons become actual weapons, capable of inflicting real damage. Bows and arrows fall into this category, once you've got steel-tipped arrows. So do air rifles—ask our feathered friends. A .22 calibre rifle, as everyone knows or should know, can easily kill you, and the smallest shotgun is murderous at close range.

So don't give these items to youngsters until they're old enough to have a solid sense of responsibility. Even then, it's up to Dad to put on a rigorous safety campaign, with lectures, demonstrations, and the strongest kind of warning that any departure from the code of safety and sportsmanship will mean the abrupt end of that particular activity.

Just Follow the Simple Instructions

IN MY OPINION, American toys lead the world, and are getting better all the time. My own Link Research Corporation, working closely with such well-known firms as Mattel, Knickerbocker and Hubley, is busily engaged in market research and the design and development of new and unusual toys and games. Due for release soon in celebration of their 100th anniversary, is a game I have developed with the Milton Bradley Company. It is to be called, "The Game of Life," and has become a Linkletter family favorite.

I have one grievance against the toy industry, however. Some day a frustrated father (I won't mention any names) is going to look up the address of a toy manufacturer, find him, shoot him down in cold blood, and be completely exonerated by a jury that won't even leave the jury-box to deliberate his fate.

The case for the Defense? It will undoubtedly go something like this:

"Your Honor, the Defendant purchased a Little Space Man's Rocket Ship that was advertised as a toy that could be assembled in fifteen minutes by following the easy instructions in the booklet. Taking it home, hiding it, and then getting it out at midnight on Christmas Eve for the easy job of assembly, this poor father thereupon was confronted by six pages of directions, the first paragraph of which I would like to read into the records of this court. "Arm E fits over Gismo G after Lever L-2 is inserted into Opening X, snugly revolving about Ratchet M except when Motor Hood moves forward past Gear Box or vice-versa." At 7 A.M. on Christmas morning, Your Honor, sweaty, disheveled, bleeding, and with parts strewn from the Christmas Tree to the fireplace, this unhappy creature was interrupted by his son, who stood there in his pajamas asking, "Are you Santa Claus's helper?"

No experienced parent in the land could help but cheer for the verdict! Innocent in the first degree!

As a matter of fact, the toy makers of the world are taking note of the rumbles of discontent and devising gadgets that really do go together easily. They have done this by the simple expedient of hanging this warning on every box: "Parents, keep your cotton-pickin' hands off the contents of this box. Let your child assemble this toy!"

Do-It-Yourself Fun

STORE-BOUGHT TOYS are fine, but an endless stream of ready-made playthings may not be the best thing in the world for a kid's inventiveness or initiative. One of my chief complaints about life in the U.S.A. is that we're all in danger of becoming spectator-automatons. To a scary extent, it seems to me, everything is being hand-carried to us in this modern age, neatly packaged, ready to use with no work, worry or thought. Whether it's food, fun, entertainment or education, the cry nowadays is to give it the production line treatment and have it ready for consumption with no effort on anybody's part.

That's why in our family we've always tried to make

the Links spend part of their fun-time in making their own toys, designing their own costumes for home-produced plays, and building or inventing their own outdoor games.

A notable instance of this is the Grand Prize competition for the most original Christmas Tree decorations in our house. This takes place each Christmas morning, before the presents are opened. Each child has his own small tree in his room, and he must make, hang and completely finish the decorative motif for that tree. There are generally just enough categories so that everybody wins something: most original, most colorful, most dazzling, most breath-taking, or just most-Most!

Do-it-yourself kits are the answer to this prayer for participation in fun, and even if Junior comes up with an eye-shaking horror that resembles a nightmare in spades, just nod your head enthusiastically and send him back to make a dozen more. Never, never, say, "What's that?" or "Please get that thing out of here!"

One great enemy of initiative in kids is (or can be) —hold your breath—television. I'm certain that I horrified the network and some of my sponsors recently when I was asked, during a House Party broadcast, what to do about a teen-ager who wouldn't study, wouldn't read, and wouldn't talk to anyone because he was anchored in front of a TV set from morning till night. "Break it!" I said, and I was referring to the TV set, not the teen-ager.

The fact is, television is the newest and most fascinating toy ever invented to bedazzle mankind. It can be a stimulus, but it also can take the most active mind and reduce it to a soggy pulp if used unwisely or too often. Television has much to offer in the way of information, inspiration, entertainment and just plain fun. But when it becomes the total way of life of a growing youngster, then it's time to unscrew the "on" knob and hide it. Better yet—burn it.

On the other hand, TV can be the most miraculous "carrot" that can be dangled in front of a rebellious kid. As a reward for good performance, it can hardly be equaled, and as a punishment it's simply great. A parent can deny a child his favorite show, and next time around the youngster thinks more than twice before risking another cancellation.

Some programs, of course, could be turned *on* as

additional punishment . . . but let's not go into that. Maybe *you'd* list House Party and People Are Funny among them.

Our Own Personal Recipe for Fun

MAYBE YOU'D LIKE a peek into the Linkletter family to see how our private formulas for fun work out.

Diane, the youngest, can amuse herself by the hour simply by arranging and re-arranging her collection of dolls, dresses and gadgets. Or she can take down from the shelf a game that involves putting something together and lose herself in the fun of solving it. Or she'll come rushing breathlessly up to me, throw her arms around the part of me nearest to her, and yell: "Let's do something together!" Whether it's a walk around the neighborhood, a game on the lawn, a swim in the pool, or a ride on our bikes, she's for it. You name it, and she's ready. Diane was born to enjoy life —and she sure does.

Sharon wants companions. She prefers games where there's give-and-take, where sharing provides the thrill. She's a great party-goer. When she's with a friend, she's happy to do whatever the other kid wants. She doesn't have to be captain or on the winning side to have fun. When she loses, she congratulates her opponent—and means it. That's something rare, even among adults. Sharon is well named: she gets her fun by sharing it—with others.

Robert is choosy. He knows what he likes, and whom he likes, and that's good enough for him. He can enjoy himself alone with a model kit or an electrical problem, and he can sit by the hour picking out chords on a ukulele or a guitar. He likes people in general, but chooses his friends carefully and sparingly. His toys run to mechanical gadgets that can be made, torn down and re-assembled as often as necessary. Just recently he's discovered the most wonderful and fascinating toy ever invented: girls. I have a feeling that he will be a collector. And that's not bad, either!

Dawn is too old for toys, now, but we remember her dolls and books because they're still around to remind us of the frantic urgency that impelled her to make each choice. Intense and almost desperate in her love for her favorites, Dawn could also show a streak of Jekyll and Hyde in her treatment of them. Nobody knew which toy would be cuddled lovingly or thrown perversely into some corner.

This year Dawn is discovering a whole new world of fun in her marriage—particularly a new (for her) type of playroom known as a kitchen. I'd love to be hiding in the bread-box when Husband John tastes some of Dawn's first creations!

As mentioned before, Jack was the original hobby kid. Nothing existed that he wouldn't collect if he could find it. And the trail of discarded hobbies left behind him resembled what I imagine was left in the wake of the Oklahoma Land Rush. But actually, all these samplings will undoubtedly prove useful to him if he stays in television. It helps if an emcee knows at least a little about a lot of things.

Lois and I have our own ideas, of course, about what constitutes fun. We like to travel, we like to be with the kids, we like to be with each other. I have my work, which I regard as fun. Lois has her weaving—the products of her big loom always amaze visitors. In fact, they amaze me.

Both of us feel that fun is a participating thing. If you don't contribute something yourself, something is missing. We've tried to pass this conviction along to the kids, and I think we've succeeded pretty well.

That's why our basement, our closets, our attic, and our garage are filled with odds and ends that can be put together by anyone with the desire for do-it-yourself fun. Pieces of costumes, decorations for holidays, and rebuilt gadgets fill boxes and drawers from one end of the house to the other. A Cave of Horrors, anyone? We have the skeletons, witches, shrunken heads and rubberized monsters for a little dandy. Re-fight the Civil War, did you say? Dig down deep enough and you'll come up with muskets, uniforms, sabres, and enough medals for all the generals (everyone *is*). Enjoy a Hawaiian luau? The torches are in the photographic darkroom, the grass skirts can be found over the old refrigerator in the pool house, and the drums, ukuleles and gourds are all next to the water softener in the basement.

Really, fun is where you make it—that could be the motto hung over the Linkletter fireplace or the legend on the Link coat-of-arms. Because if you want to have a ball, it takes only the flimsiest excuse to get started. It's the competition at the table for the best story-teller to invent a cliff-hanger that wins him the extra scoop of ice cream for dessert. It's the third anniversary of Diane's triumph over the clock, marking the moment when she could tell time all by herself. It's Sharon-dunking-time at the pool, celebrating the opening of the season when The Water Is Heated and You Can Go In Any Time You Like. Or it's a formal holiday when Valentines are sent, or Hallowe'en Witches fly, or Easter Bunny eggs are hidden.

So what we say in our house is this: if you don't have any fun around here, it's your own fault!

In Short . . .

FUN IS IMPORTANT for everyone; it's the oil that eases the friction of living. And toys are important, not just because they're a source of fun, but because they teach and help kids to grow.

The truth is, toys aren't just luxuries, as people

used to think; they're necessities for the welfare of your child. So take some trouble about them. Give them some thought. See that your youngster has a balanced variety of toys for indoor and outdoor play, toys that give him a chance to express himself, that stimulate his physical and mental growth, that fit his age level.

See that he has a reasonable number of well-made, well-planned, store-bought toys. But don't swamp him with them. Encourage him to invent his own games, sometimes, to improvise his own toys.

Teach him not to be just a passive spectator when it comes to having fun. Make him see that the most fun comes when you're most involved yourself, as an active, contributing participant.

If you can get that message across, you can paste a gold star on your parenthood rating. A great big shiny one.

Chapter 5

Ambitions Unlimited

IN THE PAST FIFTEEN YEARS or so I think I've been exposed to more childhood ambitions than anyone in history, with the possible exception of Santa Claus. It's my own fault. One of the standard questions I ask kids on my House Party program is, "What do you want to be when you grow up?" And believe me, I get some startling answers.

Some are short and to the point. One little angel-eyed charmer, I remember, said she wanted to be a donkey.

"A donkey?" I repeated, mystified. "Why a donkey?"

A smile of anticipation appeared on her face. "So I could kick the stuffing out of my brother," she said.

There was also a young man who wanted to be a cat.

"A cat?" I echoed. "What kind of cat?"

"A tom-cat," he said promptly.

"Why a tom-cat?" I asked.

"I don't know," he said wistfully, "but that's what my dad says *he'd* like to be!" A revelation that rocked the country—with delight—from coast to coast.

I believe kids start having ambitions from the moment the wheels start spinning in their busy little heads. At first these ambitions center around physical things: whatever feels or tastes good. But by the time a kid is three or four, he not only wants things that give him pleasure, he wants to *be* something that will give him satisfaction.

What he wants, of course, is to be important, even as you or I. So from the start he tends to see himself in some dramatic or heroic role: a fireman snatching people from a blazing building, a cop shooting it out with bank-robbers, a trained nurse saving a life, and so on.

I think these early ambitions are well worth noting, because quite often they give parents a clue as to the type of personality they're dealing with. An adventurous boy will want to be a spaceman, a maternal little girl will want to be a mother, an imaginative child will leap from ambition to ambition like a mountain goat. A youngster who feels close to his father will probably want to be just like dear old Dad . . . no matter what dear old Dad is really like. I remember asking one of these kids what his father did for a living.

"Nothing!" he said happily.

"Doesn't he work?" I queried.

"Nope!"

"Doesn't he like *any* kind of work?" I was trying to give Dad a break.

"Sure," said Junior. "He likes *easy* work!"

Well, that father may not be setting any worlds on fire, but at least he had a loving and loyal son. Which may be more important than making money, when you stop to think of it!

Kids love excitement and glamor and romance and danger. They're not greatly attracted by the prospect of hard work or responsibility—and being more honest than grown-ups, they admit it. We like to boast that any youngster in America can grow up to be President. Maybe so—but I have yet to find a single one who wants to be President. Too much worry! Too much responsibility. Besides, the President doesn't even get to fly his own plane.

Even more surprising than the things kids want to be are the reasons they give for wanting to be 'em. Whenever I probe for these reasons, twelve million viewers wait with bated breath because nobody knows what will happen next. I certainly don't!

The five- and six-year-olds are the most fun, because they're the most unpredictable of all. I had a typical quartet the other morning, all scrubbed and shining and fidgety. Three boys, one girl. They wanted to be, from left to right, a doctor, a lion-tamer, a movie star and a trained nurse.

I asked the budding medico why he wanted to be a

doctor. He gave me a heart-warming smile. "So I can take people apart!" he said.

I asked the future lion-tamer what he'd have to remember if he wanted to succeed with his four-footed friends. "To stay away from their mouths," he replied promptly, which summarized *that* profession very neatly.

I asked the Gregory Peck of the next generation why he wanted to be a movie star, and a blissful expression spread across his face. "I'd like the life," he confided.

"What would that be like?" I asked him cautiously.

"Well," he said, "a movie star wakes up at ten and has breakfast in bed. Then he takes a limousine to the studio and kisses girls all day. Then he has dinner at some nightclub, and if he wants to, he marries the prettiest girl late that night!"

I didn't try to disillusion him. I moved hastily on to the future Florence Nightingale. "So you want to be a nurse," I said. "What would you do if I had a terrible cold?"

"Nothing," she said.

"Nothing?" I echoed. "Why not?"

"Because I wouldn't even be there," she said serenely. "I wouldn't want to catch it!"

One convenient thing about childhood ambitions is that logic doesn't necessarily rear its ugly head. I remember one six-year-old who told me that when she grew up she was going to be a mother.

"That's nice," I said. "Will you have boys or girls?"

"Oh," she said scornfully, "I'm not going to have any *children;* I'm just going to be a mother!"

Most kids like to be asked about their ambitions; it makes them feel important, and sometimes jolts their imaginations into action. But sometimes you'll find a kid who says, quietly but firmly, that he doesn't want to be anything.

This kind of negative reaction always worries me, because I don't think it's normal. It may mean that the child has been scolded or over-corrected to the point where he's afraid to try anything new for fear of making more mistakes. It may be that he feels unloved or unwanted, and is already beginning to reject the world in which he finds himself. In any case, it's a danger-signal. Most happy youngsters are bubbling with ideas and enthusiasms.

The most startling ambition I've encountered lately came from a youngster in the studio audience the other day who said, during a brief question-and-answer period, that he had a query about juvenile delinquency.

"Juvenile delinquency?" I repeated. "All right; what is it?"

"What I want to know," he said earnestly, "is how you get *into* it!"

He wasn't really thirsting for a career of crime. He had heard his elders discussing the topic—with grim disapproval, no doubt—and had decided that anything so alarming must be pretty exciting, even if he didn't know what it was.

What Parents Can Do

I GET A LOT of letters from parents saying, in effect, "Tell us, please, what we can do to help our children achieve their ambitions." This is a big question, and undoubtedly each set of circumstances would call for a different answer. But here are a few suggestions that may be useful.

In the first place, *study your child.* The better you
know him, obviously, the more you will be able to help
him with his ambitions—or anything else. No two kids
are alike; that's what makes parenthood so challenging
and exciting and difficult. Some youngsters are slow to
develop: they're unsure of themselves; they need to be
encouraged and pushed and guided. Others seem to
know right from the start exactly where they're going,
and the best thing the parent can do, probably, is
jump out of the way.

In our household, for instance, Jack always knew he
wanted to wind up in show business. Oh, he had a thousand passing interests and hobbies, but he always kept
his eye on that particular ball. He was never afraid of
the limelight. I remember once, when Jack was about
eleven, I was supposed to be master of ceremonies at the
Electric Exposition in San Francisco. Lois took the
children down early, but I got caught in a traffic jam
and couldn't get to the big show on time. I was really
frantic; there were twelve thousand people waiting for
me. As my car finally screeched up in front of the building, I heard the theme music over the loud-speaker and
knew that I couldn't possibly reach the stage on time.
Then suddenly out of the loud-speaker came a perfectly
calm and assured eleven-year-old voice: "I'm Linkletter; the small one. My daddy's not here, so let's start
the show!"

He started it, too. So you see, we never had to light
any fires under Jack. If anything, he had too much

assurance. The problem with Jack was teaching him a certain amount of patience and self-control.

The contrast between Jack and Dawn was amazing, when you stopped to think that they had the same parents and the same environment. Jack was the type of child who, if he came up to a door and it wouldn't open, would turn the knob a couple of times. Then he'd rattle it. Then he'd pound on the door, then he'd kick, finally he'd go and look for an axe. But if Dawn tried the same door and it didn't open easily for her, she'd decide that it was locked (whether it was or not) and she'd go away. She'd accept defeat much too easily.

Kids are born different, that's all. Parents must realize this, and deal with each child as an individual. Dealing with Jack, we had to hold him down. Dealing with Dawn, we had to build her up. Both have turned out fine: Jack is a disciplined young man with a TV show of his own, and Dawn is an enthusiastic, warm, outgoing young wife of an Air Force lieutenant. But when they were growing up, they represented totally different problems, because they were totally different personalities.

I think very often young parents tend to use their first child as a sort of yardstick to measure succeeding children by. I know Lois and I did this, and it was a mistake. Jack was an unusually stable child, one who was always a couple of years ahead of himself socially and emotionally. As a result, we expected too much of Dawn too soon—and of Robert, too. It took us quite a while to learn the lesson I am preaching so glibly here: namely, to treat each child as an individual, and not apply blanket methods of child-rearing. What works with one won't necessarily work with another.

So *study your child*: that's the first step in helping him achieve his ambitions.

The second step is, *teach him that work can be fun.* This may sound like a revolutionary concept, but I have a strong feeling that very often a distaste for work is implanted in children by parents who are always complaining about their jobs or the housework or anything that requires effort. One of the most valuable gifts that parents can give a child is pride in a job well done. If Mother grumbles constantly about the necessity for dusting or sweeping, why should her small daughter find any satisfaction in tidying up her room? If Dad goes off to work every morning with all the enthusiasm of a man en route to his own funeral, why should Junior look forward to the day when he must do the same? Attitudes are as contagious as measles. One bad set can infect a whole family.

The third step is, *watch for areas of natural interest or ability and try to develop and encourage these.* The world is full of people trapped in jobs or occupations that they basically don't like—and I think this is a sad and tragic thing. No one can work well, or be happy, if his job bores him, if it is simply a grim chore that must be endured for eight hateful hours a day. But millions of people live their whole lives under just such conditions—conditions that might have been avoided if their parents had just encouraged them to open the right door.

I was terribly lucky: I knew I wanted to work with words, and I found a profession where the spoken word was all-important. So I loved my work, and because I loved it, I've been enthusiastic and reasonably successful at it.

The happiest men I know are those who approach their work as if it were their hobby, something to be done for the sheer fun of it, not just for the money involved. These lucky people don't have to escape from their work; they escape *into* it. Actually, they'd rather be working than not working (try to take a Sam Goldwyn away from movie making, or a Dr. Salk away from his laboratory!). And very often these people achieve fame or fortune without seeking it because, loving their work as they do, they're willing to work longer and harder and with much more enthusiasm than people to whom work is just a means of livelihood.

So if you can recognize in your child a spark of real interest in *any* area that might lead to a worthwhile career, for heaven's sake breathe on that spark, coax it along, try to kindle it into a flame. Don't smother or dampen it with indifference or lack of encouragement. Remember that it takes courage to try something new, and kids have to face newness every day. They have little experience to draw on, so they're unsure of themselves. They need praise and admiration.

They're also terribly sensitive to ridicule. I think sometimes parents forget this: even good-natured teasing can damage a certain type of child. Some friends of mine had a daughter who had a miserable time learning to read. They finally found out that the trouble dated from an episode where they had laughed at her first faltering efforts. They hadn't intended to be unkind. But the child didn't know that: she thought the two people she loved most in the world were making fun of her.

Even teen-agers can be thrown off the track by a thoughtless remark. I knew a boy once, quite a brilliant youngster, who took some aptitude tests that indicated strong potential legal ability. He reported this gaily to his father with the airy prediction that maybe some day he'd wind up on the Supreme Court.

The father, who had personal reasons for disliking lawyers, looked at his son disgustedly. "I'd just as soon be a mummy!" he said.

Seven words, no more. But that boy veered off from the law and wound up in a profession for which he was much less suited. At certain stages in a child's life, ambition is a fragile plant; it doesn't take much to crush it.

It All Adds Up

THE WAYS in which a parent can help a child realize his ambitions are almost endless, and it isn't just a question of sending a child to the best available school or college. Opportunities exist for character-improvement from the moment the kid begins to talk. I know some psychologists who say that a kid's success in life (or lack of it) is determined by the time he's ten years old, and I think they're probably right.

Anything a parent does to build self-confidence in a child increases the kid's chances of success. If you teach a boy to throw a baseball straight and hard, or a girl to be a good swimmer or dancer or tennis player, some of their uncertainty and timidity disappears. Nothing builds confidence like doing something well, over and over again. Find out where your child's skills and aptitudes lie and help him develop them.

Anything that teaches a youngster self-discipline or patience or persistence will pay off later in terms of earning power or job success. I remember when I was a kid in grammar school I used to pedal out on my bicycle into the San Diego back country and collect the lemons that had been discarded by the packing plants. I'd bring them home, scrape off the scales in one of my mother's galvanized wash-tubs, then organize a gang of kids to sell them from door to door for a nickel a dozen—and I'd take a percentage of one penny! It wasn't exactly big business, but it built up my self-confidence and sense of leadership. And that could have been nipped in the bud had my mother forbidden the troublesome project.

In many ways, parents sometimes do things that make it harder for their youngsters to achieve their ambitions. A mother who is too harsh a disciplinarian can create in her children a resentment of authority that may plague them all their lives. A father who brags about padding his expense account, or cheating on his income tax, may be setting moral standards so low that some day his kid may find himself in trouble with the government or with his employer, or both. Monkey see, monkey do.

Sometimes I think parents damage their children by demanding too much too soon. Nothing upsets a child more than the feeling that he simply can't measure up, that more is being required of him than he can deliver. I've known kids in school whose grades got worse and worse instead of better simply because their parents nagged them unmercifully or compared them unfavorably to children who simply happened to have more scholastic ability.

Some parents seem to expect superior performance,

not just in some areas, but all down the line. This is silly. Psychologists know that if you're loaded with ability in some directions, you're likely to be below average in others. People who are good at mathematics rarely make good linguists: they're happier dealing with numbers than with words. That's why engineers are rarely poets, and vice versa. Lawyers tend to have clear, logical minds, but not soaring imaginations. People with a high degree of manual dexterity are not likely to be found curled up with a book of philosophy. And so on. There's a kind of law of compensation operating here that parents ought to realize.

Take me, for instance. I like words, I like people, I like ideas. But when it comes to mechanical gadgets, I'm right down among the morons. If you carefully teach me how to perform some simple mechanical chore, I may stick with you through a mighty mental effort. But within a short time my mind will have rejected everything you said.

Consider my annual experience with cameras. By the end of the summer, I've painfully acquired a good deal of knowledge about light meters, shutter speeds, filters and whatnot. But each spring, when I start taking pictures again, I have to re-learn every single step. Somebody practically has to show me how to click the camera.

Same thing with household fixit problems. I am absolutely hopeless. I found this out one memorable night when Lois and I were first married. We were living in a tiny apartment with one lamp, and something went wrong with the lamp cord.

"Master of the house," said Lois, "will you fix it?" (She could have fixed it herself, but she wanted me to feel like the strong protective male.)

"Certainly!" I said.

So she brought the screwdriver and the tape and the pliers. I carefully unscrewed everything, and shaved the insulation off the wires, and put everything back together, and wound it around with tape. Then I plugged it in and—bang! The whole apartment house—in fact, the whole neighborhood went dark. They even had trouble at the main plant. So that was the last fixing I have attempted in the household in twenty-five years. I leave it all to Robert, now. He likes that sort of thing.

How to Banish Boredom

THE OPPOSITE OF AMBITION, I suppose, is apathy, or boredom. Sometimes I get letters from parents complaining of these qualities in their kids. "Nothing much seems to interest Johnny," the letter will say. Or, "Susan just doesn't seem to care about anything."

I always think that these parents ought to take a good long look at themselves. Maybe they haven't got many interests or enthusiasms either. Maybe they have them, but don't let the kids share them. Kids are like a mirror; they reflect whatever is around them. If a mother never reads to a small child, or tells a bedtime story, how can she expect the kid to love books later on? If a father never helps his boy build and fly a kite, never takes him fishing or hunting, never gets out and plays ball with him on week-ends, how can he expect the kid to be enthusiastic about sports?

The more interests and hobbies and enthusiasms a grownup has, the more likely his child is to absorb them *if* he's not pushed out of the way. ("Oh, for heaven's sake, go watch television!") Small children love to be with their parents, even if the occasion is no more exciting than a ride down to the shopping center. Older children love to be taught things by their parents: they're flattered by the attention and doubly motivated because they want the praise and admiration that only their parents can give.

I knew a writer once who made a careful study of the Quiz Kids, those brilliant youngsters who entertained millions of people for years on radio. He found that in virtually every case, one parent or the other had been almost a constant companion to the child from a very early age, sharing ideas and interests, going places and doing things together, having fun with each other.

To achieve this sort of companionship, the parent will have to learn to come down to the child's level; you can't expect a six or eight-year-old to climb up to yours. But very often a child's interests are wider than you think. In fact, there are times when I think that most of us let our parent-child contacts become much too stereotyped. We take the kids dutifully to the beach or the zoo when they might get a much bigger kick out of going with us to a play or a pawn-shop or an auction.

There are rewards in this sort of companionship for the grownup, too; being with a child you love can be rewarding in many subtle ways. Perhaps nothing note-worthy happens at all, but simply being together gives the current of affection between parent and child a chance to grow stronger. And now and then some tiny episode will occur that you never forget. The famous minister, Norman Vincent Peale, once told me of walk-ing around a farm with his youngest daughter Eliza-beth, then aged about four. A bluebird swooped down over them, and for a fraction of a second the father saw the reflection of the bird in the little girl's aston-ished eyes. "Just a flash of blue," he said, "reflected in a child's wide eyes. It was gone in an instant. But I never forgot it."

I can see why he never did.

Don't Push Too Hard

COMPANIONSHIP, interest, encouragement, guidance—all these a kid has a right to expect from his parents. But some parents don't stop at helping a child achieve his ambitions. They unload their own frustrated ambitions on the child.

We've all seen examples of this: the father who was a pretty fair athlete driving his son to become an All-American when what the boy really wants to be is a poet or a chess-player or a research chemist. The mother who tries to compensate for her own marital disappointments by interfering constantly in her daughter's marriage. The shoemaker who decides that his son is going to be a lawyer or a doctor if it kills both of them—and sometimes it just about does.

Parents often justify this intense selfishness (that's what it is) by insisting that they know what's best for their children. But it's never "best" to try to make over another person in your own image—or worse, the image of what you wanted to be.

Some of the worst examples of grafted-ambition take place right here in Hollywood, in my own profession. Show business is infested with the type of women known as "stage-mothers." These are usually neurotic females who wanted a theatrical career themselves, but never had the talent or the training or the opportunity. So they take their defenseless children, hammer a certain amount of "talent" into them, and then try to force them into show business one way or another.

The kids aren't to blame: they're no match for the ferocity and frustration pent up in their mothers. Sometimes, driven by the ceaseless pressure, they even become child stars. But they pay a terrible price. I don't see many stage-mothers any more, because word has gotten around how I feel about this sort of exploitation. But they still exist, and the damage they do is appalling.

You've got to face the fact that your kids won't necessarily share some of your own enthusiasms. My own fond dream was that Jack and Robert would be basketball players. That was my chief sport in school, and I showed them my medals, letters, cups, and pictures from the moment they could walk. I put up a basketball hoop in the back yard and practised with them. I took them to the best games I could find. I had them meet and talk with the best players in Southern California.

And what happened? Nothing! Neither of them ever played in an inter-school basketball game that I know about. They much preferred swimming and surfing. That's what they enjoyed most, so that's what they did. I'm glad of it.

In Short

IF YOU WANT to help your child achieve his ambitions, study him, watch him, listen to him. Be interested in his plans for himself, however far-fetched. Let him know you care, really care, and are on his side.

Don't worry if his early ambitions shift and fade and change. Most of us went through dozens of phases before we began to acquire any focus. I've known some very successful people who didn't know until quite late in their educational career which road they wanted to follow. Some people make a final decision even later. Dr. Smiley Blanton, the eminent psychiatrist who appeared on our House Party program, didn't start studying medicine until he was almost thirty. Before that, he was a teacher of dramatics at Cornell.

Expose your child to as many areas of opportunity as you like, but don't try to force him into any. If he shows some interest, open a channel for him if you can, but don't push him through it. Don't expect too much wisdom or realism too soon. A child is only a child; don't judge him or his ambitions by adult standards.

Where his ambitions are concerned, give your child encouragement when he needs it, guidance when he requires it, help when he asks for it and interest all along the line.

In other words, give him yourself, with love.

Chapter 6

Crime and Punishment

IF YOU'RE EVER IN A GROUP where things are getting dull, just bring up the subject of kids and discipline. Nothing will ginger up the conversation (or wreck old friendships) faster, because everybody has strong opinions and considers himself an authority. When to punish? How to punish? To spank or not to spank? Yakety-yak, far into the night.

My own views are reflected pretty well in the story of the lady who took her little darling on a shopping trip, and in the middle of a large department store His Young Highness proceeded to have a royal tantrum. Kicks, screams, roars—the works. The distracted mother stood helpless until a clerk whispered to her that the store maintained its own psychologist just to deal with such emergencies. A great authority, trained in Vienna.

"Get him," cried the frantic mother. "Quick!"

So the psychologist appeared, surveyed the horrid scene, then stooped down and whispered something into Junior's shell-pink ear. Something miraculous, evidently. The tantrum ceased at once.

"My goodness," gasped the happy and mystified parent. "That was wonderful. But what on earth did you say to him?"

"Why," replied the great expert, "all I said was, 'Listen, you little brat, if you don't stop that yelling this instant I'm going to break every bone in your body!'"

So you can easily see, in the great spank-or-not-to-spank controversy, which side I lean toward. The backside!

Obviously, there must be some control, some discipline in every life. But this sort of control doesn't spring up of its own accord. It has to be taught. A kid can't teach himself, so the parent has to teach him. If the parent doesn't teach the child self control when he's young, life is going to teach him much more harshly when he's older.

The child is going to resist this. Why not? For the first few months of life, he's allowed to act pretty much as he pleases. Then suddenly grownups begin to thwart him here, frustrate him there, set limits to activities which up to now have been tolerated. And how does he react? Exactly the same way you would react if you were in his diapers: with red-faced rage.

The Tantrum-Tossers

SOME KIDS ACCEPT frustration meekly; others simply explode. If screams and yells seem inadequate, they'll add wall-kicking, head-pounding and breath-holding . . . all designed to measure a parent's will to resist. And if the parents *are* intimidated to the point of giving in, then the kid has learned the gentle art of blackmail . . . and he'll go on using it just as long as it works.

In our family, we never had any tantrum-tossers. Jack was always too level-headed; Dawn was probably too timid, and the others—having no precedent to follow—never acquired the knack. So I can't claim to be a first-hand authority on tantrums. But to parents so afflicted, my advice would consist of the following simple rules:

1. Don't give in. In fact, make it plain to the child that tantrum-tossing removes every vestige of a chance to win a concession or gain any advantage.

2. Don't lose your own temper; one tantrum at a time is enough.

3. Don't wring your hands or display any other signs of agitation (he'll be watching you like a hawk); just pick up young Master or Miss Tantrum-Tosser, deposit him or her in a room devoid of breakables, close the door, and ignore the roars.

It's a good idea, though, to leave some small face-saving loop-hole behind you, perhaps a remark to the effect that "You can come out when you've stopped crying." Sometimes a kid will work himself into a spot where he can't abandon his bad behavior without seeming like a quitter or a coward.

The other day my friend Lucille Ball told me a story about her son Ricky that illustrates this point. Ricky, in mid-tantrum, screamed that he didn't want to see his friends, play with his toys, or do anything except what he was doing—which was yelling. A little while later, Lucy said to him, "You might as well stop being mad, because you're going to miss a lot of fun, and then you'll be sorry."

"All right," said Ricky. "As a matter of fact, I'm sick and tired of being mad right now!"

The moral is: leave the kid a ladder so that he can climb down from his high horse.

Grabbers, Snatchers and Non-sharers, Inc.

HAVE YOU EVER attended a birthday party for two-year-olds where Johnny whacks Sally over the head with a toy shovel or vice versa? Have you ever watched an embarrassed Mama try to persuade Jimmy to be a little gentleman and share his toys—with about as much success as a keeper trying to persuade a hungry leopard to go halves on his ration of raw meat at the zoo?

Sure you have, because such behavior is par for the two-year-old course. Every parent wants his off-spring to be a model of decorum. But it's silly to expect a very small child to exhibit traits of unselfishness that it took mankind half a million years to develop—and on which most adults retain only a slippery grip throughout their entire lives.

So don't be too surprised, or alarmed, if Junior's debut into society is marked by occasional earnest attempts at assault, mayhem, assassination, or even cannibalism. If he's the really aggressive type, you'll have to prevent him periodically from splitting Sally's skull, setting Stevie on fire, scalping Susie, or biting large chunks out of the new baby.

Of course, some children seem to be born gentler and more considerate than others. In our tribe, the little mother was Sharon. She was always the one who was miserable if one of the others was hurt, who comforted them when they were spanked, who was always there to soothe and love and pat them. She never complained when other children yanked her hair, stole her toys, hit her, kicked her, or called her names. She might go off and cry by herself, but she'd never come tattling to us.

There are times, to this day, when I think Sharon is the best-balanced of all of us. I know that if I have a problem, and Lois isn't around, I'm likely to take it to Sharon for a solution. In fact, I sometimes take it to Sharon when Lois *is* around!

If you have a child or children like Sharon, you're lucky. But don't despair if you seem to have produced a potential Lizzie Borden, Lucrezia Borgia, Al Capone, or Bluebeard. Sure, some kids will be tantrum-tossers and toy-snatchers at two, and profane and habitual liars at four, and self-centered and vacuum-minded at eight, and heaven knows what at sixteen.

But they'll probably get over it, and in between times they'll be as affectionate as kittens, as playful as porpoises, as unpredictable as the stock market, as lively as crickets, and as much fun as any other cliché you care to mention.

Even when they're bad, they're wonderful, in a ghastly sort of way. Ever hear of a parent who traded one in? I never did!

Such Language!

I SEE THAT a couple of paragraphs back I used the word "profane" in referring to four-year-olds. This may be a bit strong, but every parent knows that by the time they're three—or sometimes even two—kids have already learned to distinguish between "good" and "bad" words.

How does this happen? Well, I'll never forget one

youngster who appeared on our House Party program. I asked her a standard question: "Did your parents tell you anything to do or not to do on the show today?"

She nodded solemnly. "They told me not to say any dirty words."

"Dirty words?" I was surprised. "I'll bet a little girl like you doesn't even know any."

"Oh, yes, I do," she said. "You ought to hear my mother yelling at the neighbors!"

Very funny, on the air. In real life, not so funny. Because children don't just naturally start using bad language. They have to be exposed to it. And all too often the exposure takes place right in their own homes. Half the time they don't even know what the word or phrase means, but they know it has shock value. So they use it. Why? Because it gets attention, that's why.

So the best way to discourage this little game is not to react the way the kid wants you to react. Don't faint, flinch, turn pale, or act as if the heavens had fallen. If possible, look bored. Say that such language is childish, which it is. (The last thing any child wants to be considered is childish.) Then change the subject.

If the bad-word habit persists, or becomes really offensive, you may have to resort to some form of punishment. But this isn't likely to be necessary if you remind yourself that the kid is really experimenting with words, and learning that certain sounds carry more emotional impact than others. It's a stage we all went through. Ninety-nine times out of a hundred, it's nothing to worry about.

Duel at the Dinner-table

IF THE MAIL I GET is any yardstick—and I think it is—the most urgent question in America today is not what to do about the Russians, or inflation, or space travel—it's how to get Junior to eat his vegetables. This is a problem that apparently turns the dinner-table into a combat area in countless American homes.

I think the trouble starts because the kid figures out early that here is a marvelous battle-ground, one on which he can win ninety-nine percent of the victories with almost no trouble at all.

He senses that Mommy is being driven by a powerful instinct that impels her to feed her young. He knows that he can't fight her openly in many areas—she is much bigger and stronger than he is. But here is one where he can really make her squirm. She can't pry open his mouth and make him swallow his food. If she browbeats him too much, he soon discovers that he has an amazing invention right inside him—a reversible stomach. He's most likely to use this counterattack when Dad takes a hand in the war. "Eat those peas!" roars the alleged head of the house, thrusting a spoonful under Junior's shrinking nose. "Watch out!" cries Mommy in despair. Too late. Back comes everything. Field Marshal Junior has won another campaign.

There is a cure for all this, of course, that has a blissful simplicity, although the protective instinct in most parents is so strong that they hesitate to use it. The cure is simply a little judicious starvation.

I have before me a typical and plaintive note from a harassed housewife in Milwaukee. "What about a seven-year-old boy who refuses to eat anything but hamburgers? His father and I can't do a thing with him!"

It seems to me that the crux of the problem lies in that word "can't." Here are two great big grownups groveling in front of a seven-year-old because, presumably, they're afraid he'll starve to death if they take his hamburgers away. Or because they've been taught to think, somewhere along the line, that if they deny Junior's slightest whim he'll become a mass of inhibitions and repressions and grow up to be a howling neurotic.

Poppycock! What this mother should do is give her son well-prepared, balanced meals, and if he doesn't eat a reasonable amount of a reasonable number of items, let him starve! She'd be amazed to see how soon everything looked good to him. With our own Links, one skipped meal was usually enough. I've heard of some determined children who actually went an entire day without food. But by the next morning they were ready to eat nails.

As any doctor will tell you, a couple of skipped meals won't hurt a child. And it *will* prove who is running the household.

In all fairness to the kids, I must confess that I have known parents who were fanatics on this subject of food. I have never, myself, been one of those eat-everything-on-your-plate-or-else advocates. Sometimes a child may genuinely dislike a certain food. Sometimes his plate may have been overloaded by an over-zealous parent—or even one who is unconsciously expressing some resentment toward the child. Sometimes a minor emotional upset (a first-grader facing school, for instance) can render him honestly incapable of eating anything. Parents should keep these things in mind.

As for the old bugaboo about eating between meals,

I certainly don't think a child should be permitted to gorge himself on sweets whenever he feels like it. On the other hand, children can burn up energy very quickly, and when you're growing fast your body may not be satisfied with three meals at specified intervals. In our house, we never put any ban on milk or fruit or fruit juice between meals. In fact, we tried to keep them available.

It's the old question of trying to maintain an intelligent balance between the extremes of no discipline on the one hand and unreasoning strictness and rigidity on the other. Some parents are too quick to pounce. Like the father I heard about the other day who observed that his four-year-old wasn't eating her supper.

"Sally," he said ominously, "you've been eating between meals."

"No, Daddy," she said. "I haven't."

"Look me square in the eye, young lady!"

"I can't, Daddy," she murmured sadly.

"Aha!" he said triumphantly. "And why not?"

"Because," she said demurely, "you haven't *got* square eyes, Daddy."

Which ended *that* discussion very neatly.

I think it's a pity when food and its consumption becomes a great issue in a household, because it tends to spoil the few daily occasions when members of a family naturally get together. Lois and I always eat supper early so that we can be with the kids. There's no place in the world like the dinner table for family discussions, family plans, the telling of jokes or minor adventures or even a little good-natured teasing. It was at mealtime that we developed our family game of far-fetched continued stories, each story teller leaving the hero or heroine in some cliff-hanging predicament and passing the buck to the next person. We found it a wonderful way to develop imagination in youngsters, and discourage self-consciousness.

The dinner table, too, is a great training ground for manners, the little disciplines that don't come naturally to kids, but which they must learn sooner or later if they're to be acceptable members of society. A nodding acquaintance with "Please," "Thank-you,"

"Excuse me," can be implanted without too much effort at family meals.

So if the family dinner seems to be vanishing from your home in favor of hasty snacks or trays in front of the television set, get it back. Encourage the kids to express themselves freely, when their turn comes (the old saw about children being seen and not heard is for the birds). Have an iron-clad rule that bans quarreling, bickering, arguments, reading, TV watching, or radio listening. Pay attention to just one thing: each other. You'll be amazed to find out how much fun it can be.

Tall Tales and Small Liars

QUITE OFTEN my mailbag contains questions from anxious parents whose uneasiness stems from the fact that their offspring have strayed from the narrow path of truth. Not once or twice, but many times. And they want to know what I think about this.

Well, to begin with, I think that none of us tells the whole truth the whole time—and that we'd be pretty unpleasant to have around if we did. I think furthermore, where children and falsehoods are concerned, you have to distinguish between the truth-boosters and the truth-dodgers.

The truth-boosters are those electric youngsters who are so full of imagination and vitality that plain old dull reality isn't good enough for them. They have to liven it up a little. Like the young man of seven who was on our House Party program not long ago. I asked him a standard question: "What's the funniest thing you ever saw?"

You could almost hear the wheels in his head begin to whir. "Yesterday afternoon," he said, "I heard a rap on the backdoor, and when I opened it this funny thing was there waiting to come into the house."

"Funny thing?" I prompted him. "What do you mean?"

His eyes grew wide. "Well, it had the feet of a horse and the neck of a lion and a body like a cow's and . . ."

"What was its tail like?" I thought we had better get to the end of this creature.

"Like a fish!"

"What did you do with it?" I thought this might slow him up.

"I brought it in and introduced it to my dog!"

"And what did your dog do?"

"He ran out of the house and I haven't seen him since."

"Well," I said helplessly, "where is this thing now?"

"It's home," he assured me, "watching us on TV!"

I gazed at him sternly. "This is all true, now, isn't it? Not just imagination?"

"Sure, it's true," he said indignantly. "And I don't know what a 'magination is. I don't think we've got one."

He was no liar; he was just a truth-booster, and a good one. All children have this vivid streak of make-believe in them. Some of them visualize things so intensely that they really can't tell where reality ends and fantasy begins.

Some have remarkable insight. The other day I asked a young lady of six to describe her conscience for me. Her answer came out in a rush, with no time for punctuation: "It's a gray ghost inside you with a friendly face but it stops smiling when your nerves begin to write a note to it when you want to do something bad and when the ghost sees this bad note he gets very angry and yells 'Stop!'"

Can you give a better definition of "conscience"? I can't.

The truth-boosters are fun to have around. But the truth-dodgers are a little different. They are the kids who distort facts, not for fun or amusement or entertainment, but for their own advantage, or to avoid criticism or punishment.

Nobody likes this kind of dishonesty or evasiveness, and parents are right to worry about it when it appears more than occasionally. But they should also ask themselves, I think, whether perhaps the youngster hasn't been subjected to *too* much pressure or discipline somewhere along the line. If a child is frightened enough of the prospect of punishment, he will lie or evade or do almost anything to avoid it. And since he is too young to be a very skillful liar, many of his lies will be transparent and obvious.

We were always pretty firm about the importance of truth-telling in our household, and tried to make it clear to the kids that—no matter what the crime—the penalty would always be worse if they lied about it. But trying to look at the problem from the child's point of view, I can see now that a sensitive youngster like Dawn, who wanted her mother's approval more than anything in the world, would do almost anything to avoid the loss of that approval. So if Lois asked her sternly if she had been crayoning on the wallpaper, poor Dawn must have felt an overwhelming impulse to say that she hadn't. Not because she wanted to be untruthful, but because she didn't want her mother to stop loving her.

Parents forget, sometimes, that kids haven't had time to develop a strong sense of right and wrong. A ten-year-old, let's say, takes fifty cents from her mother's purse and buys candy for all the kids in the block. Technically, this is stealing, and certainly it should be discouraged. But it's at least possible that the child's mind was so fixed on her good motives (generosity and pleasure-sharing with her friends) that she thought of nothing else. Or perhaps she felt that, since this was "family" money, she had some right to it. Or maybe she figured that, if her mother had been home, she would have asked and received permission to take the money.

The point I'm making is simply that it is much more difficult for a child to distinguish between right and wrong than for a grownup, who has had several decades of experience. But very often we grownups judge the child's action by adult standards. And this simply isn't fair.

To Spank or Not to Spank

SOMETIMES, OF COURSE, a child will deliberately do something that he knows perfectly well is wrong, or cruel, or dishonest. Then something must be done to convince him that this sort of behavior doesn't pay. In other words, punishment becomes necessary, and this puts the parent squarely on the spot. If the punishment is too weak, it will have no effect. If it's too strong, it can affect the whole parent-child relationship, or even damage the child's personality. No wonder some parents become so confused that they alternate between spinelessness and flashes of severity and harshness—probably the worst of all climates for child-rearing.

What such parents need to realize is that children not only need discipline, they want it. No matter how much kids seem to resent authority, they resent even more being left with none at all. For a child, the feeling that there are no restrictions, no rules, no controls can be terrifying. He interprets it to mean that nobody cares . . . and sometimes he's right!

Quite a few years back, I remember, a friend of mine sent her eight-year-old boy to a very progressive camp, one of those places where Junior was supposed to express himself freely and do pretty much as he pleased. All seemed to go well except for one odd thing: Junior kept writing home and saying that he needed another pair of sneakers.

After the mother had mailed two or three pairs, she finally dispatched her husband, with yet another pair, to visit the camp. Dad asked Junior why he kept losing his shoes.

"Well," the youngster said uneasily, "we have a game we play now and then. We see who can throw his shoe farthest into the lake."

Dad's reaction to this happy bit of information was to take one of the new sneakers and apply it vigorously to the area where he thought it would do the most good. Junior shed a few tears, but not many. "Gosh, Dad," he said, when the storm was over, "I'm glad *somebody* feels that way about it!"

Not only do children sometimes welcome punishment, I think that very often they'd rather have it swift and to the point than face a ceaseless verbal barrage. Parents who nag their children constantly are being much more unkind than those who enforce rules, occasionally, with a little judicious palmistry. I'll never forget the sad-eyed little girl who was answering my questions on House Party one morning.

"How old are you?" I asked her.

"Five," she said.

"And how old would you like to be?"

She thought a moment. "Nine thousand."

"Nine thousand!" I said. "That's pretty old. Why would you like to be that old?"

She said, bleakly, "Cause then I'd be dead."

"Why do you want to be dead?" I asked, startled.

"Because it would be so peaceful," she said. "Mommy wouldn't be screaming at me all the time."

It was a chilling little bit of dialogue. I only hope that Mommy was listening—and got the point.

Education, some philosopher once said, begins at the bottom—of the child. Do I agree? In some cases, yes. I don't believe in beatings. I don't believe in straps or hairbrushes or switches. But with some children, at certain times, a good smart slap on the backside is the quickest and most effective way to cut through the layers of selfishness and inconsiderateness that are making the child behave like a monster.

It's hard to generalize, because the decision to spank or not to spank varies with the temperament of the child, the degree of wilfulness, the nature of the crime, and so on. But here are a few suggestions based on my own experience and (I hope) common sense:

• In the first place, never spank a child when you're in a towering red-faced rage. For one thing, you may over-do it, hit harder than you intend to. Furthermore, the child knows perfectly well that *you're* out of control—precisely the crime you're punishing *him* for. And this won't increase either his love or his respect for you.

On the other hand, I wouldn't advise any parent to be completely cold-blooded about punishment either. There is something pretty repulsive about the deliberate infliction of pain, devoid of all emotion. Be angry, in other words, but make sure your anger is under control.

• In the second place, don't spank for trifles. The crime should be a major one; it should have been committed deliberately, not by accident; the child should know exactly what he is being punished for, and why.

• In the third place, the spanking should be carried out as close to the behavior-lapse as possible. This is particularly important in the case of small children, who have short memories. With older children, especially boys, mothers are apt to say, "Wait until your father comes home! Then you'll get it!" Sometimes, in such cases, the delay and resulting apprehension may legitimately be considered part of the punishment. But I don't think all punishments should be handled by one member of the parental team. It tends to create an ogre in the family, and reduces the authority of the non-punishing parent.

One of the silliest things parents can do is change horses in mid-punishment. Nothing confuses children more than to have a punishment decree laid down by one parent altered or reduced by the other (nothing makes the first parent madder, either). I have a friend, the father of many, whose wife sometimes meets him at the door with a shrill cry of "Your son has done it again!" (It's never *his* son when the good grades arrive.) The wife thereupon demands summary punishment upon the body of the offender, locked in his room. The husband builds up a big head of steam, rushes upstairs, unlocks the door, and lets Junior have the first spank. Whereupon there's a yowl from the wife that echoes all over the neighborhood: "Stop killing my baby, you brute!"

Some day, this will end in justifiable homicide.

Spanking, of course, loses its effectiveness as a child reaches the age of reason, and should no longer be necessary, in my opinion, by the age of eight or nine. Spanking a teen-ager has to be an actual beating if it's going to make any impression—and who wants to punish that severely? I can easily think of a lot of delightful tortures to administer to a wayward teen-ager, including a total curfew on dates, the abrupt drying-up of the fountain of allowances or pin-money, and the elimination of favorite pastimes that are likely to range from movies to television to fancy foods or special parties.

In Short . . .

THE LIST of possible crimes is endless, and so is the list of punishments, but let's not pursue it. What I've been trying to say is that, while punishment is never pleasant, there are times when it's a necessary evil. That judicious punishment isn't cruel—it's really kind. That children need and want a framework of discipline inside which they can grow and develop happily. That they are miserable without one.

Finally, I think it all-important that punishment should be balanced by affection, and that soon after it has been necessary to punish, the parent should find a way to reassure the child, remind him that he is a treasured part of the family, make him feel that his parents' love for him is still there, unshaken, unaffected by the transgression, however serious it may have been.

Loving discipline doesn't hurt a child; it helps and strengthens and reassures him. The parent who can blend these two ingredients—love and discipline—in the right proportions will find all the other problems of child-rearing simple.

Even better, he'll find them fun!

Chapter 7

The Tempestuous Teens

IT WAS MARK TWAIN, wasn't it, who used to remark that in his opinion, all growing boys should be kept in a barrel until their seventeenth birthday, with only a small bunghole through which to breathe and be fed. "And then. . . ." He would pause to light a cigar.

"And then what?" some eager listener would cry.

"Why, then," the creator of Tom Sawyer would say, blowing a reflective cloud of smoke, "the bunghole ought to be sealed up permanently, of course!"

So you see, teen-agers have been taking quite a verbal beating for quite a while.

Let me confess right away that I like teen-agers and sympathize with them most of the time. This is partly because I can look back through the mists of time and distantly recall being a teen-ager myself. And partly because for the last ten years we've always had a teen-ager in the house—and with Sharon and Diane coming along we have at least another decade to go.

Everybody admits that the years between thirteen and seventeen are tricky and tough. Physically, a kid is going through all sorts of drastic changes designed to turn a girl into a woman and a boy into a man. Emotionally, he's likely to be baffled and confused by the new problems that come crowding in on him. All the nice, stable relationships of his childhood seem to be changing. Part of him still wants to be guided and protected, another part resents his parents, rebels against authority, wants to break away. School gets tougher. Sex rears its fascinating head. Time-tables of one sort or another become terribly important. When to start lipstick, high heels, dating? What about curfews? What about smoking and drinking—those dubious symbols of adulthood? What about cars? What about almost everything?

No wonder teen-agers get so self-conscious. No wonder the general speed-up of modern living hits them harder than anyone else. No wonder, when everything around them seems to be changing, they hate to seem "different" themselves. I mentioned earlier how Robert shrank from the glare of publicity that inevitably falls on an entertainer's family. For a while, there, if the family went for a walk, Robert would lag twenty paces behind so as not to be recognized or stared at. As I mentioned before, he even asked me once if he couldn't change his name from Linkletter to Jones or Smith. I told him, as gently as I could, that there were advantages as well as disadvantages in being part of a family like ours, and that changing his name wouldn't really change things very much. But he wasn't kidding; he was going through a phase where he was so unsure of himself that he didn't want to be noticed.

There's no doubt that in this day and age kids mature earlier than they did a generation ago. Or *seem* to mature earlier. When I was in high school, a fifteen-year-old girl who wore lipstick was practically a fallen woman. Now they start at twelve. When I was in high school, nobody—or almost nobody—owned a car. Now anyone who doesn't is considered a little square. All the experimenting we did with drinking, smoking, smooching or what-have-you is now done much earlier . . . sometimes with not very happy results. Because while customs have changed, human nature hasn't. Kids don't grow up much faster emotionally than they ever did. So your modern youngster is forever being pushed into situations that he really isn't ready to handle and this makes for discord and confusion all down the line.

Memoirs of a Rolling Stone

I'VE BEEN LUCKY all my life, and even as a teen-ager I was lucky because fate, or circumstances or something, decreed that just about when I was ready for it, physically and mentally, I was plunged head-first into an experience that was as broadening and toughening as a teen-ager could possibly have had. It might easily have been *too* toughening: I wouldn't recommend it as a standard part of teen-age education. But in my case it worked out pretty well.

It came about like this. I finished high school a month before I was sixteen. I was too young for college, and I knew it. Most of my classmates were a year or two older than I was, and I was still rather undersized physically. So I decided to wait a year before going to college, and in that year get out of the nest, try my wings, and see if I could find out what made the world tick.

This was a rather ambitious attitude for a teen-ager, but I honestly felt that if I knocked around a bit I'd have a better idea of what to study at college and what to do with my life. I was fond of my foster parents, but they were so absorbed in their religious life that I felt they wouldn't miss me too much. As a matter of fact, their religious faith kept them from standing in my way: they had perfect confidence that their prayers would keep me from harm.

And so, in June of 1929, with ten dollars in my pocket, my parents' blessing, and an unsinkable supply of self-confidence, I set out to see the world. I was gone a year and a half.

My travel plans were simple: I would hitch-hike or ride the freight trains. In high school I'd done a good deal of ride-thumbing around Southern California and had learned to be a pretty fair judge of both cars and people. Riding the rails was something else again. It was dangerous and illegal, and I was lucky never to get into serious trouble.

The main reason that I never wound up in jail or in trouble was that I had a profession that I carried with me. By this time I had learned to be an expert typist. This meant that I could always find work. I might arrive in town with only a quarter in my pocket, but I would head straight for a typewriter agency. They almost always had requests on file for temporary help. If they didn't, I would simply look in the want ads.

The fact that I hadn't learned shorthand didn't bother me too much. Once, I remember, I applied for the job of private secretary to a doctor. I spent the night before my first day on the job working out a system of abbreviations and symbols, but the doctor dictated too fast. I tried writing his letters in my own way, but this was not what he had in mind when he advertised for a secretary. So we came to a parting of the ways.

Looking back, I must confess I am somewhat appalled at my own brashness. On one occasion, applying for a job in a bank, I got a book from the library and tried to master double-entry bookkeeping in one afternoon. I have an idea the people in that bank are still trying to untangle the mistakes I made. Another time I tried to pass myself off as an electric arc-welder. Under the questioning of a suspicious foreman, I conceded at first that I might be a little rusty. Then I admitted

I hadn't done any arc-welding since high school. Finally I confessed that my total experience consisted of something I had once read in a book. The foreman was so impressed by the combination of my innocent face and awful lies that he finally gave me a job in the clerical department.

All this time I was growing bigger and stronger physically, and building up reserves of experience and self-confidence that were to last the rest of my life. I think the main lesson I learned was that you can always get by if you're willing to work, and aren't too choosy about it. Maybe the work isn't exactly what you want, but one thing always leads to another, and once you've made a little money you can always move on.

I moved, all right! I worked in practically every state in the Union. In St. Paul I hung up raw meat in a packing plant. In Chicago I was a bus boy. In South Dakota I was a harvest hand. I worked in offices and factories, big business and small. Once I shipped as cadet on a freighter bound for Rio. Even there, my typing helped. The captain had a lot of letters to write, so I typed my way to Rio while my less fortunate shipmates swabbed decks or chipped paint.

I must have met thousands of people in my wanderings, but few made any permanent impression on me. Perhaps the only one whose example I decided *not* to follow was the boss I had when I was working in the National City Bank in New York. I was there in October, 1929, when the market crashed. After that first shock, you remember, a lot of people thought it had dropped as far as it could go.

At this point my boss took all his savings, mortgaged his home, cashed in his life insurance, and bought a certain stock. Since he was a canny old Scotsman who never before had invested a penny in anything, I was so impressed that I took the $196 that I had saved up during my sojourn in Wall Street and bought one share of the stock myself.

Four years later, when my wanderings were over and I was almost through college, I sold that share for eight dollars. That taught me a lesson, all right: never put all your eggs in one basket. I learned the lesson so well that, last time I looked, the business enterprises I'm involved in numbered nineteen, ranging all the way from a toy concern in Los Angeles to a sheep ranch in Australia.

I'm well aware that these teen-age experiences of mine were anything but typical, but the lessons I derived from them are lessons that I have tried to pass on to our youngsters, one way or another. So let me summarize them briefly here:

Education. Rubbing elbows with dish-washers, ditch-diggers and other unskilled workers, I had plenty of opportunity to listen to an endless, sad refrain that ran: "Oh, if only I had more schooling!" The more I saw of the turbulence and uncertainty of life, the more I wanted some security, some stability in mine. And my months on the road made it crystal clear that this sort of security and stability depended ultimately on education—higher education. So believe me, when I did go to college, I was ready to appreciate it and take advantage of it.

Experience. The second lesson I learned was that there is really no substitute for experience, and the wider the experience the better. When I went to San Diego State College, I found that my training in the school of relatively hard knocks had not only enabled me to catch up with my classmates physically, it had put me ahead of most of them in assurance and versatility.

I had almost no money, but I was used to this and found it no handicap. I lived on campus with various families where I was often chief cook, baby sitter and general handyman in return for room and board. In addition, I worked as YMCA switchboard operator, summer lifeguard, cafeteria bus boy—and for a while I was a live art model for a group of painters in Balboa Park, a chilly but financially rewarding occupation. I also made extra money by reading term papers and examinations for professors. In the meantime, I managed to maintain a high grade average, captain the basketball team, play a lot of handball and do a lot of swimming.

I could never have maintained such a schedule if I hadn't had those eighteen months of matching my wits —such as they were—with the world.

People. In the course of my wanderings I met just about every type of person under the sun, and came to a conclusion that I still hold: namely, that ninety-nine per cent of the human race are honest, well-meaning, friendly folk who will give you a helping hand if they think *you* are honest. The other one per cent ranges from people who are indifferent to anything but themselves down to those who will cheerfully damage you if they can. I remember all too vividly the time a friend of mine and I were cornered in a boxcar and robbed at knife-point by a couple of professional hobos who would have thought nothing of slitting our throats. At that end of the spectrum, you find individuals who are more animal than human, and it's silly to pretend that they don't exist.

But people in general are fine—and fascinating. No matter how much you study them, you never begin to know all about them. This applies to kids, too. You can visit their secret world, but you can never map it all. That's why exploring it is such a challenge, and so much fun.

I learned many other things from my teen-aged Odyssey. That it's highly desirable for a youngster—boy or girl—to learn some skill that will support him in an emergency, a skill that can't be taken away from him or affected by changing conditions. (In my case, this indispensable skill was typing.) That you can go anywhere and get by if you're willing to work—and are not too finicky about it. That nothing is really ever wasted: every experience contains *something* that is valuable and that can be used later. That self confidence leads to success, and that success strengthens self confidence.

As I said, I've tried to pass some of these lessons along to our own Links. But I've also tried *not* to fall into the error of assuming that everything that was good for me as a youngster would necessarily be good for my kids. Jack might have benefited from a teen-age experience like mine. I'm pretty sure Robert wouldn't. You have to remember that times change, conditions change—and no two people are alike.

That's why there's never been any fool-proof formula for child-raising—and never will be. But we *can* learn a great deal from the experience and the counsel of others.

The Silent War between Generations

LET'S FACE IT, there always has been a certain amount of friction and misunderstanding between generations and there always will be. Inevitably, kids reach a point where they resent having their parents tell them what to do. Just as inevitably, parents get fed up when the kids make a sudden grab for the privileges of adulthood without showing any eagerness to assume any of the responsibilities. In a lot of families, misunderstanding and lack of communication make matters worse. Sometimes it borders on a state of undeclared war.

Nobody is ever going to resolve *all* these differences. In fact, if parents and kids ever fully understood one another, both sides would probably die of shock. But let's take a few typical areas of combat and see if we can find some middle ground without both teams yelling "Kill the umpire!"

Judging from the mail I get, and the questions I'm asked by indignant characters of all ages who buttonhole me on the street, there are four main storm-centers where parental authority clashes head-on with teen-age desire for independence. There are countless minor points of friction: allowances, curfews, and so on, far into the night. But the Big Four are drinking, smoking, sex and cars.

As the embattled father of five and foster father of many, let me give you my views for what they're worth, plus a few clues as to how we have handled these problems in our home. I also want to make a side-excursion into the subject known as "But everybody's doing it." Let's start with the simplest of these problems (if you can call any of them simple!) ; let's start with cars.

Trouble on Wheels

IN SOME FAMILIES the battle begins when Junior starts begging to drive before he's reached legal age. The answer to this is—or should be—simple. One word. No. Any parent who can't say no to this proposition and make it stick, shouldn't be a parent. Any other answer not only encourages disrespect for law, it is flirting with the crime of murder.

Only yesterday I read of a thirteen-year-old in Chicago who took the family car without permission and decided to drive it to St. Petersburg, Florida. He got as far as Georgia. There he lost control of the automobile, hit a telegraph pole, and decapitated himself. It might have been even worse. He might have hit a car full of innocent people.

Even when they've reached the legal age to hold a license, statistics prove that teen-agers are all too often a menace behind the wheel. They *should* be superb drivers; they've got the night vision and the depth perception and the reflexes—all the physical equipment. And some of them are good: skilled and careful. But their record as a whole is pretty dismal.

At least six million of the eighty million drivers on the road are teen-agers, and the majority of these six million love speed and excitement and the feeling of power that a big, humming engine gives them. Most of them have a blind faith in their own ability to stay out of trouble. Some tend to be contemptuous of anyone who drives with caution.

Right here in California, not long ago, a study made by the Highway Patrol showed that close to 35 per cent of the state's teen-agers were habitual speeders. Their rating was much worse than average in such unpleasant areas as drunken driving, failing to yield right of way, improper signals, driving on the wrong side of the road, driving with faulty equipment, and so on.

The National Safety Council figures that teen-agers are involved in twice as many fatal accidents for the number of miles driven as drivers who are 25 or older. That's a pretty grim picture. We still need a lot of education somewhere along the line to convince these youngsters that, when it comes to killing people, a car is a lot more dangerous than a gun.

In our family, I taught the older kids to drive when they became eligible for a learner's permit. For this we used a small blue Henry J. Kaiser sedan, known affectionately as Henry. Henry had his troubles—once somebody put sugar in his gas-tank, which made him very unhappy. Another time, when our nurse was driving him, he had a collision that bashed in his front end. The nurse went into a near-by house to report the mishap by phone to Lois. "I'm all right," she said, "but you should see poor little Henry!" The lady who owned the house was convinced a child had been mangled. She almost fainted.

Henry was a good teacher, though; neither Jack nor Dawn have had any traffic troubles. When he got his first TV job, Jack bought a car of his own. But he was so afraid that it might get scratched that he often came home and borrowed Henry, if any sort of rugged driving was involved.

By that time, Jack was in college. He didn't own a car while in high school because—I may as well go right out on a limb on this—I don't think high school youngsters are old enough to own cars. It gives them too much independence, too much freedom of action. And it has a grim effect on their grades. Survey after survey has shown that, once he owns a car, your average A student will become a C student. A C student will become an F student. A college student may have developed enough stability and self-discipline to do his work whether he has a car or not. But the average high school teen-ager hasn't. The temptation to goof off and go driving is too much for him. He shouldn't be exposed to it.

A lot of traffic experts around the country are getting increasingly worried about the problems posed by teen-age drivers. The authorities are getting tougher about cracking down on violators and suspending or revoking licenses. But the real solution to the problem lies inside the home. If parents would teach their kids to drive carefully and conscientiously, if they would insist on respect for traffic laws and traffic courtesy, if they would establish an iron-clad family policy of good driving or *no* driving, the roads of America would be a lot safer. And so would America's kids.

"But Everybody's Doing It!"

WHERE YOUNG TEEN-AGERS are concerned, a lot of parents get thrown off their disciplinary balance by a gambit that is as old as the pyramids. When a thirteen-year-old or a fourteen-year-old wants to do something that is against the family rules, they raise the plaintive cry: "But Mother, everybody else is doing it!"

More than once, when Lois and I probed a little

deeper into the situation, we found that "everybody else" was busy complaining to their parents about the same restriction, and insisting that Jack (or Dawn or Robert) Linkletter was doing it.

So there are times when a little note-comparing among parents is very much in order. Otherwise, there's no telling where this kind of log-rolling will end.

Once in a while, of course, it turns out that most of the kids in the gang really are permitted to do something which has been taboo in our household. When this happens, Lois and I usually talk the problem over. If we think the activity is harmful, or definitely out of line, we continue to forbid it. On the other hand, if it's a relatively minor matter, we may revise the family rules. Teen-agers hate to be different; they need the security that comes from being a member of the pack. It's not fair to a kid to make him feel like a lone (and put-upon) wolf.

Smoking and Drinking

WHAT TEEN-AGERS WANT more than anything else is to be grown-up, to cease being children. So naturally anything that symbolizes adulthood becomes attractive to them. It may be high heels, lipstick, dating, or driving a car. It may be smoking. It may be drinking. It may be going steady. As I said before, most youngsters are reaching for these things years earlier than their parents did. And this can easily lead to tension and friction in a household.

I've always thought that teen-agers respond better to persuasion than to command. Arbitrary rules handed down without explanation annoy them—sometimes to the point where they'll go out of their way to break them. If you make a kid feel that you think he's capable of listening to reason, then he'll listen to it. But after he reaches a certain age, he likes to feel that the final decisions are his.

As a matter of fact, they are. After a kid is fourteen or fifteen, a parent can only advise—he can't really compel.

When Jack got to the age where most of his friends were smoking, or were about to begin, I remember we had a couple of talks. Nothing very solemn. Just casual man-talk. We agreed that it was rather nice to do what everybody else was doing. But I pointed out that leadership and conformity didn't always go together. In fact, I said, the thing that set leaders apart was always a degree of *differentness*.

I said that in my own case a strong deterrent, where smoking was concerned, was my desire to be a good athlete. When I was growing up, it was accepted as gospel that athletics and cigarettes didn't mix. This, plus the fact that I never had any money for non-necessities, kept me from picking up the habit. So I didn't smoke, and I had never regretted it.

Jack thought this over for a while, and decided not to smoke either. Dawn made the same decision, and I think probably all the kids will. It's partly parental example, of course. But I also think it's because we never made a great issue of it, never laid down any iron-clad laws, once they had reached the age of reason. We left it up to them, and their common sense said No.

Since 1952, of course, a great deal of evidence has been presented adding up to the strong probability that heavy cigarette smoking is a definite health hazard. Not only where lung and throat cancer are concerned, but in many other areas. It's too early to tell whether filters eliminate the danger. If a parent wants to discourage smoking in a youngster, I think he would do far better to present some of these medical findings in a calm, objective way, than to preach or threaten or make a great moral issue of the whole thing.

Where smoking is concerned, you've got to remember that teen-agers are bound to be impelled by a certain curiosity as to what it is that makes half the adult population spend six billion dollars a year for cigarettes. This curiosity leads most of them to experiment, then the desire not to be different persuades them to continue the experiment until the smoking habit is formed. And once the habit is formed, as everyone knows, it is not easy to shake off.

I think many people derive a lot of pleasure from smoking, and I'm well aware that it is a billion-dollar industry giving employment to thousands of people.

Because of network contracts, I've had tobacco sponsors for one of my shows. But I have never said that I smoked, or allowed myself to be shown with cigarette in hand, pretending to smoke, because I thought it would be dishonest. I don't smoke, and Lois doesn't smoke, and the Links don't smoke—and I'm glad of it.

We're not much interested in drinking, either. We never drink unless we have company, and then it's a ceremonial cocktail before dinner, and that's it. If we give a party (and we almost never give large ones), no guest who over-indulges is ever asked to our house again. We see no reason why the kids—or ourselves—should be exposed to bad manners or vulgar language or the off-color jokes that seem to gather momentum when people drink more than they should.

Again, with the kids, it has been our policy to get across the message of moderation by example and casual conversation rather than grim lectures, threats or penalties. I read somewhere not long ago that a survey of problem drinkers and alcoholics showed that a high percentage of them came from homes where liquor had been identified with deadly sin and forbidden with rigid strictness. I think that might well be true: too much pressure can bring a sharp reaction—in the other direction.

Medical science is making new discoveries about the problem of alcohol all the time, and the more a teenager knows about the facts the better. Your average teen-ager has a great respect for science. He may not listen if you tell him that all the great religions of the world frown on the excessive use of alcohol. But he may prick up his ears if you tell him that there are five million miserable alcoholics in the U.S.A. today, that two hundred thousand people become addicts each year, that nobody can predict who the victims will be, and that his own chances of becoming one—if he decides to drink—are one in fifteen or sixteen, which is a gamble worth thinking twice about.

I go very light on drinking myself because I don't need any stimulant to have fun out of life. Actually, scientifically speaking, alcohol isn't a stimulant: it's a toxic depressant. People who get very gay and merry after a few drinks aren't really being stimulated. Their inhibitions are being removed as the higher centers of the brain become affected. But actually they are being drugged. An alcoholic is a drug-addict. I have known a few in my time, and believe me, it is a pathetic and terrifying business.

I think, myself, that if family life is gay enough, and fun enough, if there's enough love to go around, enough mutual support and affection, then alcohol isn't likely to become a problem because what it has to offer is only second-best—and a poor second-best at that.

That's the way Lois and I feel about it, anyway. And I'm pretty sure the Links do too. People who have to have alcohol to have a good time seldom have as good a time as people who don't. It's as simple as that.

Smooching, Going Steady—and Beyond

My views on the ancient and venerable practice of smooching can be summed up in one short paragraph:

Let's face it, teen-agers are going to smooch somewhere, somehow, with some one. We all did. Trying to stop it would be like trying to stop the earth from revolving around the sun. So the best thing for a parent to do is relax and depend on what he's put into his child's character during the last fourteen or sixteen years. If the right attitudes aren't built in by that time, they never will be.

The truth is, by the time a modern youngster reaches his teens, he probably knows as much about human reproduction as his parents—maybe more. Perhaps he got it, somewhat distorted, through the grapevine. Maybe he was lucky enough to have parents who handled his questions frankly and sensibly as they came along. Maybe somebody handed him a book—there are some good books designed just for this. Maybe he dug his information out of libraries. Or magazines—some of our big women's magazines go into details that would have jolted the hoop skirts right off our great-grandmothers.

Actually, I think a certain amount of frankness is a good thing because it tends to lift sex out of the furtive, smutty category where it stayed for so long and label it for what it really is: a magnificent gift from God that is meant to be used but not abused. If parents try to keep sex hush-hush, and make a great mystery of it, a child is quite likely to develop an abnormal degree of interest in it simply because it's taboo.

Teen-agers are going to be interested in sex no matter what their parents do, because nature is busy pumping them full of a whole new set of hormones designed to make them interested. Studies by Kinsey and others have pretty well established the fact that in their late teens boys are at the peak of their sex drives and capacities. As Dr. Joseph H. Peck says in his colorful book, *All About Men,* "During adolescence, your boy has the soul of a poet and the carnal appetites of a tomcat, so it's no wonder his judgments are as erratic as his emotions."

This being the case—and it is—I can easily see why parents spend a good deal of time worrying about the custom of "going steady" that seems to have become part of our national scene. I think, myself, that most "going steady" arrangements start innocently enough, and stem from nothing more sinister than a desire for companionship and security in a teen-ager's lonely and constantly changing world. It's a lot more reassuring for a girl to know she has a fixed partner for a party, picnic, or dance than to wonder if she's going to be a wall-flower. It's easier for a boy to know somebody is going to hold his hand and "belong" to him than to wonder if maybe the girl he asks for a date or a good-night kiss is going to wound his super-sensitive ego by saying no.

But if a young couple is together constantly, you know darn well that they're going to experiment with sex, and each time a little further along the line. As the uninhibited Dr. Peck puts it: "The one great law in sex play is progression; each time the boy begins where he left off last time, and he goes as far as the girl will let him. If he doesn't make progress each time, both of them will be disappointed; and if they go steady it won't be long before there are no more worlds left to conquer."

I am inclined to agree with the good doctor. Take the sex drive of the boy, add curiosity and a desire to please on the part of the girl, include a car for transportation to a dark beach or a lonely road, mix well, and what have you got? Trouble, that's what. Trouble with a capital T that rhymes with P that stands for pre-marital pregnancy—which is *really* a mess.

It's a mess because chances are there's no good solution. Abortion is illegal, immoral and dangerous. If resorted to, it can leave emotional scars that can interfere with later marriage. Shotgun marriages in such circumstances seldom work out well; statistics show that such a marriage is more than twice as likely as a "normal" marriage to end in divorce. Having the baby out of wedlock involves social condemnation, plus the heartache of adoption or the stigma of trying to raise a fatherless child. Sometimes, of course, marriage and a "seven months baby" works out well. But even so, it's a high price to pay for the doubtful privilege of going steady.

What to Do?

I THINK PARENTS who worry about their kids and sex would do well to realize that sexual morality is just one part of over-all morality. If you've been teaching the kid honesty and responsibility in all phases of life from the beginning, he'll apply those standards when it comes to sex. If not, not. Sex becomes immoral, it seems to me, when it is used for selfish pleasure only, with no thought of the consequences, or possible consequences, to the other person or to society as a whole. This doctrine of responsibility may seem like a complicated notion, but it really isn't. Any teen-ager can grasp it if it isn't forced down his throat in a highhanded, preachy, or dictatorial sort of way.

If parents can get this sense of responsibility across to the kids, plus a kind of family pride that certain things just aren't done by this kind of family, then they've just about got the whole thing licked.

Of course, there are specific things parents can do. Adequate sex instruction at appropriate ages all along the line. Enough activities and interests to keep the kids busy and give them channels for the energy seething in them. And so on. But the main thing, as I said earlier, is what you have put into his or her character during the first fourteen or fifteen years of life.

Sometimes the indirect approach works best with teen-agers. If you disapprove of going steady, for instance, don't gnash your teeth and rant and scold and forbid. Let Dad tell Junior what fun he had when he was chasing half a dozen chicks at once. No female was able to reduce *him* to domesticity at sixteen. Let Mother recall the fun she had playing Dad off against three or four other admirers, the jealousies, the quarrels, the excitements. . . .

Maybe it'll work. Maybe not. At least you'll have fun remembering!

In Short . . .

TEEN-AGERS ARE COMPLICATED, moody, unpredictable, often self-centered, and at times maddening, but they're also human. They're trying to grow up, so they resent arbitrary rules. They no longer consider themselves children, so they like to be consulted. They are not always lovable, and they know it, and this frightens them. They often need reassurance, and don't know how to get it.

So be patient with them, and don't expect miracles. Ninety-nine times out of a hundred there's a cure for all their troubles. Time. Where would we be without it —the helping hand of good old Father Time?

Chapter 8

My Mailman Brings the Darndest Things!

As you can easily imagine, my mailman is a busy fellow. Twice a day he totters in with a truck-load of letters which he dumps on the groaning desk of Lee Ray, my faithful secretary who would have had a nervous breakdown long ago if she could just have found the time.

But I get a tremendous kick out of my mail. It's an endless and fascinating panorama of America: hopes, fears, gripes, cheers, laughs, squawks—the works.

Lots of the letters contain questions that were designed for Solomon but got to me by mistake. Some I can answer only in my head—it's safer that way.

From a big, bold Texan: "*Dear Art, how can I get my wife to give me more of my pay-check?*" (Cash it yourself, Bub, and try running the family for a change.)

From an embattled teen-ager: "*Dear Art, why are*

my parents so square?" (Maybe they haven't been around, Junior.)

From a lady in Cincinnati: *"Dear Art, why is it that every time I come into contact with a psychologist they are always lying down?"* (What *sort* of contact, lady?)

From a harassed father in Pasadena: *"Dear Art, I have my mother, father, sister, brother-in-law and their three children here on vacation visiting us, and my daughter loves to brush her teeth with all their toothbrushes—what should I do?"* (Hide your own toothbrush, Pop.)

But a lot of letters, especially the ones about kids, expect and deserve a serious answer. So let's reach down into a typical day's mailbag, pull out a handful more or less at random, and see what's on the minds of American parents and kids from coast to coast. This technique of giving advice is a little like shooting from the hip while riding on a roller-coaster, but I'm willing to try it if you are. Ready? Let's go.

Parents Have Their Problems

HERE'S A NEEDLE-POINTED query from Minneapolis to start us off. *"Why is it that children of child psychologists always are the ones that are most in need of psychiatric treatment?"*

Well, sir, I can't go along with that word "always."

I think it's likely that some people expect a child psychologist's kids to be perfect, and react with gleeful surprise when they're not. I also think it's possible that some of these children, knowing that they're being watched and judged, react like some preacher's kids and behave like little hellions. It's even conceivable that in some cases the psychologist is so busy trying to help other parents that he can't find time to be a good father to his own kids.

But "always" off base? No, I can't buy that.

Next, a Chicago woman rather tartly inquires, *"Why do boys like to shoot holes in windows with air rifles?"*

For one thing, Madam, it makes a lovely sound. But seriously, a streak of violence and destructiveness runs through everyone, young or old. Just as some women can't resist the chance to dig their claws into some other woman's reputation, so occasionally a youngster will be unable to restrain himself when he sees a particularly inviting window or streetlight at just the right range to be challenging to air rifle, sling shot, or good right arm.

On People Are Funny recently we introduced a man whose job it was to smash slightly defective plates, cups and saucers. He gaily threw them against a cement wall we had built on the stage while I interviewed him about his job, his home life, and so on. He assured me that he never quarreled with his wife, children or neighbors, because by the time he got home at night, all the violence had worked its way out of his system.

I then wondered out loud if anyone in the studio audience would care to experiment with this kind of job, and we were almost mobbed with people of all ages who clambered on stage to smash, break, throw and pulverize the stacks of dishes.

Oh, yes, there's violence in all of us—not just in small boys with sling-shots!

A mother and dad from Chicago ask a very difficult question: *"Our two boys, aged 8 and 12, hate Sunday school and there's a big fight every week about it. Should we make them go?"*

This is a subject that I have deliberately avoided discussing in this book bcause I have found in my quarter-century of public appearances that religion and politics can only lead to arguments that accomplish little. Each family has its own salvation to work out according to the way that Mother and Dad worship. Some believe in a strong, ritualistic church. Others feel that you can worship by yourself in your own way whether you happen to be in a church or in a subway. But everyone should certainly be given the opportunity to learn about God, and then make up his own mind as to the kind of religion he wishes to practise.

Therefore, I say that youngsters should be strongly

encouraged in every way possible to attend Sunday School and church services. A Bible should be in every home, and prayers a regular part of family life.

But even a religion can become unpleasant if it's "force fed." My father was a "lay" minister and the most devout man I have ever met. I was made to read the Bible by the hour when my dearest wish was to be out with the gang playing "Run Sheep Run." I attended church three times a week, and twice on Sunday. Our prayers at each meal were so all-inclusive and lengthy that I can scarcely remember a hot bite of food passing my lips until I ate away from home. As a result, I instinctively rebelled as any child would.

So I guess that my advice to the Chicago parents is to treat the subject with understanding, moderation, and example. Try to make religion and the existence of a Supreme Being something warm and meaningful to your children. Hold out some reward for them if they do go to Sunday School, because I am sure that any small bribe is worth the eventual happiness that religion can bring. Meet with the minister of the church and tell him your problem. He will have a far better answer than any I can suggest.

Here's a Florida mother at her wit's end with a would-be wit. *"Why does my son try to twist every bit of correction into a joke?"*

This is another clever juvenile "theft" of a grown-up's evasive action. What adult hasn't tried to laugh off a mistake or an embarrassing experience? When Mother bawls out Dad for not opening the car door for her when their friends are looking, doesn't Father laugh and say, "They'll all be glad to know we're just as married as they are"?

Of course, this is no answer to the lady's problem. She is evidently faced with a smart-alecky young man who has found that he can baffle Mom with these flip retorts. I would consider that under these circumstances, a wisecrack merely compounds the crime, and would advise her to get punitive before the kid gets worse.

However, the consoling thought comes that this is a "phase" that most kids go through. Our Robert is almost fifteen, and has given us a solid year of attempts at joking his way out of trouble. Just the other night he came home from the beach where he'd gone without permission. Sensing the gathering clouds of doom, he flipped: "Dawgone it, I haven't any sense of direction. I made a wrong turn coming out of school, and before I knew it, there I was up to my neck in the Pacific!"

This extraordinary gambit, I might add, did not hasten the return of his portable transistorized radio, confiscated on the spot by an irate parent—me!

As I mentioned, I was an "only" child myself, so I was especially interested in this query from a woman in Pasadena: "*How can you keep from spoiling an only child?*"

The best way I know is to see to it that he is around other children as much as possible, and they'll see to it that he isn't spoiled! In addition, encourage him to join various groups—church groups, clubs, any social organizations like the Boy or Girl Scouts—when he reaches the appropriate age level. At Christmas time, have him go over his toys and pick out some to give to underprivileged children through some worthy cause, such as the U. S. Marines' "Toys for Tots" drive. In our house, we tried to teach the five Links about sharing by adopting half a dozen war orphans through the years, sending them toys, clothes, food and our love.

If there's only one youngster in your home, get substitute brothers and sisters in the form of relatives' children, neighborhood children, or schoolmates to visit and be a part of your household for as long as convenient. Also, encourage your "only child" to go and visit them whenever he can.

Tennessee mothers have their problems. Here's one where *"our child, aged three-and-a-half, blames all his mistakes on an invisible Mr. Elephant. What shall we do?"*

Elephants? That's strange. Here in California it's the ostriches who knock vases over and eat up all the cookies. I understand in Michigan it's bears. In Mississippi they're having trouble with the alligators. As a matter of fact, any child who can conjure up an elephant out of thin air is 'way ahead of me. It cost me a thousand dollars, recently, to fly one from India, and I'm still answering requests from kids who want it for their playrooms.

So if your child can find any extras, will he please send them on?

I dropped this letter—along with my teeth—when I read the opening sentence: *"Dear Art, I have 28 children, but I'm not married. . . ."* The answer to her problem was made easier by the next few lines: *"I am their teacher. And I'd like to know how to prevent their parents from making up phony excuses when they are absent for pleasure purposes."*

This may seem like a pretty specialized problem, but actually this question lifts the lid on a box full of explosive ethical problems that eventually confront every parent. What happens when Junior begins to compare the things he sees and hears grownups do and say with the rules of conduct laid down for *him?*

Any mother who writes a fake excuse for Mary when school is being skipped so that the family can go to the beach is going to be lied to, in turn, when Mary wants to skip a family dinner for reasons of her own.

If parents must write phony excuses, I think they might as well stimulate their child's imagination and ingenuity at concealing the truth by some unusual and intriguing story, such as: "Please excuse Mary from school today so that she can attend the coming out party we are throwing for Uncle John, who has just been released from San Quentin after serving only seven out of ten years for embezzlement!"

Here's one from a harassed parent that turns up in the mailbag at least ten times each week: "*How do you get a fourteen-year-old to do his homework?*"

There's a wise old proverb to the effect that you can lead a horse to water but you can't make him drink. This applies here. No one has ever been able to *make* a youngster think about his homework. You can put it in front of him, chain him to the desk, barricade the doors, tempt him with prizes, threaten him with catastrophe, plead for the family honor, call up his grandmother, deny him his birthright.

But nothing can make him absorb his homework if his mind is busy with Suzy Jones, the skating rink, the new cocker spaniel down the street, the monster show at the matinee next Saturday, the joys of snapping bubble gum, or how wonderful it feels to sneeze.

Just like the old Chinese water-torture, where the

constant drip, drip, dripping of the water finally wears through the victims skull, so the parent must alternately cajole, beg, and threaten until one happy day the kid looks up brightly and says, "Hey, this stuff is kind of interesting!"

In the meantime, all the parents can do is hope it happens that way before the erosion wears through *their* skull, and they are led off to a room behind bars.

How many parents have been pushed past the boiling point by an experience similar to this Glendale mother's? *"What do you do when your child insists on having the last word even though it's under his breath as he slinks away?"*

I'll never forget the time a top marriage counselor on our House Party program told us of the number of marriages that break up, or almost collapse, because of the insistence of both partners on having "the last word."

"Last Wordsmanship" is an old game first played by Adam and Eve. So don't be too surprised if heredity, instinct or imitation has caused it to pop up in your own little angel. Besides, it's not altogether a bad thing. It shows he has a spark of real life in him. He's trying to fight back against the Big People who always think they're right because *they* get in the last word— and loudly.

So don't begrudge Junior an occasional sneaky retort under his breath. Overlook it. Pretend you don't hear it. At least often enough to let him have an occasional small triumph. It's good for his soul. And if you "take" it once in a while, it'll be good for yours.

Of course, now and then a kid gets the last word in all innocence. Like the eight-year-old I heard about the other day who was reading the newspaper while her parents were entertaining guests. All of a sudden she looked up with a puzzled expression. "Daddy," she said, "what color is a paternity suit?"

My spies tell me that Dad is *still* groping for a reply.

Here's a disgusted Dad complaining about a son who is not the Davy Crockett his father remembers himself being at the age of ten: *"I'm afraid my son is a sissy. He won't go to camp with the other boys. He's afraid of the mountains even though I tell him there's nothing there to hurt him."*

Mister, don't *tell* him . . . *show* him! It's perfectly normal and natural for a ten-year-old to picture bears, lions, crocodiles, dinosaurs, and long-haired madmen behind every dark tree in the forest. So long as he's not *going* there, he can also picture himself killing, trapping, and skinning any of them. But the thought of *being* there far from home and parents . . . at night . . . is something else again. And if he happens to be the imaginative youngster who can *really* dream up a menagerie around the tent, I don't blame him for not wanting to go.

Besides, this is a heaven-sent chance to take him yourself and get acquainted with Nature together. It'll bring you both a lot closer to each other, and you'll find out things about each other that should start the kind of companionship every Dad dreams about and few achieve.

As much as Lois and I enjoy traveling, we'd give up every memory of far away European and Oriental places for the fun we've had just a hundred miles away in the High Sierra Mountains. There, year after year, we've taken the little Links on camping trips that included sleeping out under the stars in bedrolls, exploring caves, and horseback riding through strange, trailless valleys.

Starting at the age of seven, we include them in our plans for two week trips into the high country. The laughs at each other's misadventures, the tears of adversity and skinned knees, the warm sharing of emotions around the campfires, and the exhilaration of catching the biggest trout all combine to form the true definition of "togetherness." At no other time in our family history have we all been so truly together. Jealousies, bickering, selfishness, and timidity are all forgotten out where the tall trees and the high vault of Heaven make all of us seem properly insignificant. Problems that seemed insurmountable appear petty in this perspective . . . and memories are stored up that will one day be priceless family heirlooms.

Sometimes, I think, a problem can be a blessing in disguise. From Boston, the mother of a hot-rod-happy boy writes: *"What do you do to get a boy's mind on serious things instead of just cars, cars, cars!"*

This lady doesn't realize what a wonderful opportunity she has. A boy who goes daffy about anything has handed his parents "leverage" that, used properly, can get him to do just about anything they want.

Get this kid a set of do-it-yourself automobile tools, scrounge around until you find a broken-down jalopy, tow it to a place where it can be parked and worked on, and you have the perfect "weapon" to persuade Junior to do his homework, comb his hair, be polite, save money, go to Sunday school, and even get to meals on time.

Inevitably the mailman brings me a question from the anxious mother who asks, *"Do you think sex should be taught in high school?"*

If the teachers really want to know about sex, I suppose there's no harm in their asking the students! Seriously, sex education is well handled in most high schools, with a scientific approach and a lot of emphasis on the penalties that can follow the misuse of sex.

In our family, we handled the problem by answering questions truthfully when the kids asked them. We also found it useful to have pets—dogs, cats and birds—whose reproductive activities made the whole subject seem natural and un-mysterious.

With small children, I think it unwise to rush or force sex education, because it only puzzles or bores them. Recently a six-year-old startled his mother by asking how to spell sex. Naturally, she asked him why he wanted to know. "I got to write a sentence for school," he said. "Bugs are insex!"

I think the maddest Lois ever got with me was one day on the beach when I was being interrogated by an eager group of eight-year-olds—boys and girls. One asked me where babies came from, and I explained that they grew in a special place inside their mothers.

"But how do they get there?" came the inevitable question.

At this point, I saw Lois approaching. "Ask that lady over there," I said. "She'll be glad to tell you." And, like the coward I was, I dove into the sea and swam half a mile off-shore. I never did find out what Lois said to the kids. All I know is that she didn't speak to me for a week.

It was a dirty trick. I was wrong. If it ever happens again, I'll do it differently. Next time I'll swim a *mile* off-shore!

Out of my mail grab-bag comes a complaint from a mother in Milwaukee: "*How can I convince my twelve-year-old daughter that it's better to practice her flute than to play baseball with the boys in the street?*"

Try the old carrot-and-donkey technique, Mother. If Missy knows she can play baseball *only* when she's mastered her flute lessons, I think you'd see some amazing musicianship. Just tell her that the sooner she tootles, the sooner she'll be shagging flies in right field. No fluting, no fielding!

Now a sixty-year-old lady from Flint, Michigan, asks this leading question: "*Do you think children should be spanked in 1959 the way they were in 1909?*"

Well, as I've already indicated, I think the target area should be the same. But the lady implies, I'm sure, that spankings were much harsher fifty years ago . . . and I guess they were. Oldtimers among my friends seem to recall the hairbrush, the woodshed, the razor strop, the willow switch, and in school the ruler across the fingers. Sometimes they even seem to enjoy the memory.

But this has gone out of fashion now, and I'm glad of it. Somehow, the use of any object in hitting a child seems heartless to me. Spankings in our home have usually been a slap or two on the backside to command attention for the pointed lecture that followed. Like every parent, I've had my moments of sharp regret following a spanking where I hit harder than I meant to. And more than once I've even apologized to the victim for being carried away by the occasion.

Some of the questions the mailman brings me reflect family problems that are unnecessary, that shouldn't exist at all. Here's one from a Pittsburgh matron that gave me cold chills: *"How does a mother discipline her child, once that child is married and has a baby of her own?"*

I guess some people are like quicksand . . . once they've got something or someone in their grasp, they never want to let go. In this case, I hope that the "child" has been lucky enough to marry a traveling salesman whose route takes him to Seattle and points west. And that she travels with him. Because only in this way does this woman's "baby" stand a chance for happiness.

If she still needs discipline at this point, it's too late for Mama to supply it. Life will have to take care of it.

Kids Have Their Headaches, Too

ALL THESE QUERIES, so far, have been from parents. But kids have their problems, too. And a surprising number put them in stamped envelopes addressed to A. Linkletter, Hollywood, California.

A lot of the problems seem to center around those two-legged ogres known as parents. Here's a note from an indignant fifteen-year-old siren: *"When I go out on a date, my father has a trick of setting an alarm clock at a certain time. I am supposed to get home in time to turn it off. Otherwise, he wakes up, and I am in trouble. What do you think of this?"*

Young lady, I think you've got a very smart Dad. I wish I had thought that one up myself! If more fifteen-year-olds knew that they had to get in at a decent hour or else, the juvenile homes would be a lot less crowded.

Speaking of penalties, an Alabama girl reveals her age with this tremulous question: *"Is a thirteen-year-old too old to spank?"*

Yes, I think she is. Any mother and dad not imaginative enough to figure out something more effective and lasting than the back of their hands aren't spending enough time and thought being parents. Any physical punishment for a teen-ager has to be an actual beating before it makes much impression—and who wants to punish that severely? There are better ways of imposing discipline: the abolition of TV, of movies, of pin-money, and so on.

Oh, the woe and anguish we suffer when we are fourteen! An indignant Miss sputters: *"What makes par-*

ents think they have the right to listen in on an extension to their daughter's private telephone conversations?"

I don't believe most parents think they have the right. A parent's first duty to a child when he accidentally picks up an extension phone and hears a private conversation is to hang up. It's unthinkable for him to eavesdrop; he should be embarrassed at the very thought of it.

I know. Because I'm embarrassed every time I think of the things I've heard!

Here's another question involving privacy: *"When you have your boy friend over, how can you keep your little brothers or sisters from trying to "get into the act?"*

This is something for parents to handle. No little

boy or girl ever drew breath who didn't scheme how to eavesdrop on their older brother's or sister's romance. No fellow who ever called on a girl wasn't blackmailed in some way by the bratty kid sister or brother so that he could have some privacy for smooching.

Just as the diary, letter box, desk or bureau drawers of a youngster should never be disturbed by other members of the family, so a person's right to entertain company without someone giggling under the couch should be insisted upon by parents.

The automobile, of course, has just about eliminated the front parlor as the natural arena for pre-marital jousting. But in the early teens, when the family jalopy is not available, then the pests of the tribe should be grabbed by the scruff by Dad and hung out to cry somewhere else in the house.

A girl from Oakland writes: *"Do you think it is okay for an eighteen-year-old girl to smoke? My father strictly objects."*

Here's a dad who's asking for trouble. If an eighteen-year-old girl goes around with boys and girls who are smoking, and if she really wants to smoke, he might just as well forbid the tide to come in. And in the meantime, he will cause unhappiness and conflict, not to mention ultimate deception and disobedience, in his home.

I think sometimes that my own non-smoking goes back to a humiliation suffered when I was about thirteen. Somebody gave me a package of chocolate cigarettes. I thought it was a real pack, and hastily hid it in my pocket until I could assemble my gang in the shed. There I announced proudly that I had acquired some cigarettes, we all got matches ready, and I passed out the "weeds." You can imagine what an idiot I was voted when they not only wouldn't draw—they melted!

Here's a plaintive wail from an eleven-year-old. *"Why don't grownups like comic books?"*

The truth is, a great many do! But most parents object simply because so many so-called "comics" are not funny at all, but simply trashy adventure or horror stories. I've addressed myself to my offspring more or less in these terms. Be honest, now, kids . . . how many actual laughs do you get out of a comic book? If it's adventure or excitement you're looking for, there are libraries full of great stories written by men and women who could make the English language sing.

If this sounds stuffy, then make the most of it! Good stories, well written, are more real *fun* than the junk that's ground out under the label of "comics."

Let's take a letter from the bottom of the pile. Here's a twelve-year-old with a straightforward question: *"What do you do if your parents do not give you enough allowance?"*

Young man, you have just joined the largest club in the world! You are a member of the biggest pressure group ever seen outside of Washington. No twelve-year-old of my acquaintance has ever been given enough allowance except perhaps the son of the fabled Texan who was accosted by a friend: "What's this I hear about your twelve-year-old flying his own plane?" "Shucks," replied the oilman sheepishly, "it's only inside the house!"

Here's one, complete with photograph, from a cute little twelve-year-old in Atlanta. *"I was asked to go steady. My mother thinks I am to young. I love this boy. What should I do? (1) Sneek (2) Say no to him."*

I'd have to go along with Mother on this one. Don't (1) Sneek. Tell your Romeo: "Later, 'gator."

Here's another that might not be such a wisecrack as it appears at first glance: *"What's a parent for?"*

Apparently this boy, aged thirteen, has had so little guidance or companionship from his father and mother that he's genuinely bewildered as to their real function . . . outside of providing bed and board.

On the other hand, it's possible that he wants to know what parents are *for* since they've only let him know what they're *against.* This is something that every parent might ponder. It's all too easy to become a totally negative parent, surrounding your child with a picket fence of "don'ts."

This next question, in one form or another, has been asked by generations of kids: *"How do you get your parents to like rock 'n roll?"*

In other words, how can a youngster get parental

interest and understanding for a fad that older people seem unable to enjoy. When I was a teen-ager, the question would have been, "How can you teach your parents to like rumble seats?"

All this reflects the ancient puzzlement in which the older generation wonders why kids aren't the way they were, and the younger generation is convinced that older folks are a bunch of hopeless mossbacks who can't understand them.

Nobody is ever going to be able to eliminate this barrier completely. We just have to crawl under it or jump over it or squirm around it as best we can.

My right hand reached unconsciously for the scruff of a young man's neck when I picked up this next letter: "*Why do my parents always say, 'Ken are you coming along with us?' Oh, I love that! I want to go where I please.*"

Here's the whine of an ungrateful pup whose parents are trying to include him in their plans as part of the family. Even if he doesn't relish what Mom and Dad are going to do, he should at least be happy to be part of the gang. "Belonging" is one of the strongest of all human needs and desires. But here's a young snip disdaining the precious sharing of love, fun and companionship.

Here's a question from a bewildered and possibly resentful fourteen-year-old girl: "*Why don't some parents want their children to grow up?*"

I think that many parents regret seeing the years flit by and dread the approaching departure of their "brood." When a child is fourteen, any discerning mother knows that in four or five short years she won't have a child any more. And so sometimes the parent unconsciously tries to retard the development of independence in the child.

Some parents, too, re-live their own youth by watching their kids live theirs. Somebody once said, "Youth is such a wonderful thing. It's a pity it's wasted on young people!" Maybe parents like this are enjoying this exhilarating and precious feeling through the children, and hate to see it escaping them *again*.

Here's a problem that many parents never even suspect. It comes out of a note from a twelve-year-old in New Mexico: *"How do I say I'm sorry when I've done something bad?"*

It's difficult to say, "I'm sorry," even when you're fully grown. For a kid, it's often almost impossible. And so this wistful question turns up again and again in my mailbag.

Many times, I think, a child seems sullen and unrepentant when actually he's just tongue-tied, confused by the desire to apologize and the inability to put his apology into words.

Parents can help by saying that *they* are sorry, whenever they have a chance. And we all do. Because no parent ever lived who didn't regret a hasty slap, or a cold "No!" to some harmless request. In such cases, a warm and human "I'm sorry" from Mother or Dad would open the door to tender and loving sentiment in return.

In short . . .

THE PROBLEMS PEOPLE HAVE are endless, and so are the questions people ask. But the fact that they do ask so frequently and so earnestly is a good sign, I think. It means that they *want* to break down the barriers that are keeping them apart, they *want* to understand one another, they *want* to be closer together.

No one can give them all the answers. But sometimes all they want is a little encouragement and a thimbleful of common-sense. That's what I've been trying to offer in this book.

So let's end this safari through the Linkletter mailbag with a querulous cry from a ten-year-old in Lincoln, Nebraska. *"What,"* he wants to know, *"does a parent expect in a kid?"*

That's easy, Junior. We parents expect a child to be honest, brave, loyal, patient, kind, truthful, well-mannered, unselfish, intelligent, hard-working, punctual, frugal, loving, forgiving and saintly.

In short, all the things that we are not!

Chapter 9

How to Raise a Solid Citizen

EVERY PARENT WANTS HIS KID to have material success in life: to make a comfortable living, to achieve a happy marriage, to avoid the mistakes the parent made. Every parent wants his child to *be* a success, too—to grow up to be admired and respected. What can the parent do about this?

He can't do everything, that's for sure. Some things are beyond his control. He can't put musical ability into his child if it isn't there, or make a slow-witted kid bright. He can't change the heredity the child was born with. But he *can* do a lot when it comes to forming attitudes—the attitudes that will determine much of the child's later performance in life.

Psychologists say that these attitudes are implanted very early, and I think they're probably right. In the first ten years of his life, a kid is very impressionable, very easily influenced. From ten to about fifteen, he can still be influenced, but his character is hardening. After the child is fifteen, I don't think the parent can do much but put his faith in past training—and pray!

In this chapter, I'd like to list the attitudes that I think are important when it comes to getting along in this complicated world of ours. In forty-seven crowded years of living, I've noticed that the happiest and most successful people are the ones who somehow have acquired these attitudes. And conversely, the unhappy and unpopular people are the ones who somehow have missed out on them.

I don't claim that there's anything infallible about this list, or that it's a complete one. But if a parent can get most of these concepts across to a kid before the child's personality sets like cement, then the parent will have done the job he was put here to do.

He will have supplied the necessary springboard. How far or how high the kid jumps will then be up to him.

1. *A Sense of Appreciation*

I LIST THIS ATTITUDE FIRST, because it is one of the hardest to instill in a youngster. Kids have a strong tendency to take things for granted. Their imagination isn't fully developed, so it seldom occurs to them that things might be vastly different from what they are.

But American kids are fantastically fortunate. They are born and raised under the glittering canopy of the highest living standard in the world. Their health is protected by medical facilities unmatched anywhere. Basic education is assured to all of them. Unless there is some national catastrophe, they will never know hunger or want—or even unemployment.

Vast sums are spent for their amusement and entertainment. If you glance at your typical college freshman, watch him drive his car to classes or water-ski behind his own runabout, watch him surveying the whole vast field of arts and sciences with perfect freedom of choice as to which he will pursue—well, if you have any imagination at all, you can see why the rest of the world regards us with glassy-eyed wonder and envy and admiration.

This is a fabulous country, and most kids born in it are guaranteed a fantastically privileged childhood. The question is, how to make Junior appreciate all this?

It's a question that has haunted me, because my kids are so much better off—materially speaking—than I was as a child. They've grown up with servants, cars, a swimming pool, with all the toys and amusements and conveniences in the world. I suppose I could have denied them all these things, but that, I think, would have been extremist and foolish. I earned them; I wanted the kids to share them. But I've also done my best to make our Links realize that they were very lucky, that in a sense they hadn't earned any of these advantages, and that therefore they were obligated to higher standards of performance and behavior than kids who had been less fortunate.

One custom we've had in the family for a long time is my habit of writing notes to the kids. It started when I began getting more and more involved in my career, and sometimes didn't have the time for the talks I wanted to have with the youngsters. I might get home late, with something on my mind, and find that they'd gone to bed. So I'd sit down and bang out a message on the typewriter in my den, and then next morning the target of my thoughts would find one of these "growing up" letters propped on his or her bureau.

Recently I discovered that Jack had saved most of his. So here's a condensed version of a communique to him, the gist of which probably went, at one time or another, to all the Links:

"When I was your age," I wrote to Jack, "I had to get up at 4 A.M. to fold newspapers in order to earn the money for a new suit. I had to hitchhike in order to see the world. I had to work my way through college.

"You haven't had to do these things because your father has made enough money to pay for them . . . but everything in life has to balance. If you can get a full night's sleep—which I couldn't at your age— you also have to be more careful about what you do when you're awake.

"We Linkletters live in a glass house. Lots of people read about us, look at us, wonder at us. If there's a crowd of ten kids getting into mischief, no matter how innocent the caper, it will land on the front page because a Linkletter is involved—and you know who will be blamed? Not you, but your mother and me! Everyone will say *we* never taught you to behave . . . Do you think it's quite fair to let outsiders think we're the sort of parents who never do anything for their children?"

Maybe these notes didn't have the polish of Lord Chesterfield's letters to his son, but the fact that Jack saved them shows that they made some impression. And the message I was trying to get across was simply: *be appreciative. Be grateful.* Not just for the material pleasures of life, but for life itself, for the privilege of being alive, of having front row seats at the greatest show on earth, the show that Balzac called the human comedy.

If you, as a parent, can get this notion across to your child, even partially, it will greatly enhance the kid's chances for later success and happiness. Because appreciation brings with it a sense of obligation. And in the last analysis, the happiest and most successful people are those who become more aware of their obligations to other people than of their own personal pleasures and desires.

2. "*I Keep Six Honest Serving Men . . .*"

THE SECOND ATTITUDE I have tried to encourage in the Links is nothing but plain, old-fashioned curiosity. The inquisitive person is an interested person. And an interested person is an alive person.

A poem of Kipling's that has always appealed to me starts out:

> "I keep six honest serving-men
> (They taught me all I knew);
> Their names are WHAT and WHY and
>   WHEN
> And HOW and WHERE and WHO"

And the poem ends with a humorous reference to the poet's small daughter who, he says, employed:

> "One million HOWS, two million
>   WHERES,
> And seven million WHYS!"

So if you find your three-year-old diligently dismantling your ancestral grandfather clock to see what makes it tick, or thoughtfully dunking your electric razor in the toilet bowl to see if it will run under water, you should praise the Lord, even as you warm his bottom, because he has one of the greatest of all gifts—the gift of natural curiosity.

It's a gift, I think, that parents can foster in countless ways. If you have a burning interest of your own, expose the kid to it—enthusiasm is a contagious thing. I've known fathers who formed close and lasting ties with their sons in the process of initiating them into the chilly mysteries of duck-hunting. Same thing with fishermen. Or even stamp collectors.

I think a certain amount of natural curiosity exists in children just as it does in kittens. But it needs to be encouraged. Most interests grow when there is some one to share them with. So if your small daughter shows a flicker of unusual interest in—say—shooting stars, buy her a simple book on the wonders of astronomy. If she takes to that, go out with her into a field or onto a beach some night and see if you can trace a few constellations together. Sometimes, in the course of encouraging a child's curiosity, you develop some of your own.

It's a great thing, this attitude of curiosity, because the quest for knowledge always leads to a desire for still more knowledge. As his horizons widen, the curious child will begin to see how the great areas of knowledge fit into one another, how the history of the past illuminates the present, how art and architecture and literature and music and science all contribute to the wonderful world we live in.

So if the spark of curiosity is there, do everything you can to coax it into a flame. The more curious a child is, the more eager he will be to learn. And the more he learns, the more effective a person he is likely to be.

3. *The Glue of Persistence*

THE THIRD ATTITUDE IN MY LIST is not one that comes easily to kids, or to grownups, for that matter, but it is of the utmost importance if any worthwhile goals are to be attained. It's what our grandparents used to call stick-to-it-ive-ness.

It's a mistake to expect any kid to show much of this at first. A small child's attention span is short. He's not able to concentrate on one thing for very long—and shouldn't be expected to.

But, one way or another, he needs to develop this capacity as he grows older. Genius, somebody said, is nothing but an infinite capacity for taking pains. That's just a fancy way of saying that persistence is the quality that counts. And it's true enough: to achieve any significant degree of success or recognition in life, a person has to keep plugging away in the face of disappointments and failures and apparently endless obstacles.

One way to develop this attitude in a child is by timing his development properly. If a kid is introduced to problems that he's ready for, mentally and physically, and is given a little help in handling them, then he builds self-confidence as he goes along. He begins to think of himself in terms of success.

But if he's handed too much too soon, or if he isn't given adequate help, then he may find that he can't cope with his problems. If this goes on, he may begin to develop a feeling of self-distrust. And if this becomes really acute, then the kid will start refusing to do anything that's new or challenging. He would rather do nothing than tackle something that involves the risk of another failure.

I think all kids need to feel, at least occasionally, the pride and satisfaction that comes from accomplishment. More than once, Lois and I took one of the Links out of a school where standards were very high and put the kid temporarily in a school where competition was less severe, just so that he could achieve success more easily and could find out what it tasted like.

If you can slowly build in the child the feeling that he can cope with any problem, within reason, then he'll be willing to stick at it longer without getting discouraged. He figures that sooner or later he'll lick it.

But if you constantly expect more of him than he can give, then his self-confidence will dwindle, and so will his stick-to-it-iveness.

Here, again, parental example can be all-important. If you have little persistence and patience yourself, if you tend to quit on things easily, don't blame your child for doing the same. He'll just be following the leader—and the leader is you!

4. *Live and Let Live*

THE FOURTH ATTITUDE that Lois and I have tried to pass along to the Links is tolerance—tolerance of other people's beliefs and ideas even when they differ from our own. No child is born prejudiced. As the song says in *South Pacific*, they "have to be taught to hate."

I think, myself, that racial and religious prejudice are slowly disappearing in this country, but they die hard. The reason for this is probably that everyone has his disappointments and frustrations, and the resulting anger in everyone is always looking for a target. If a kid is brought up in a family where Dad hates Catholics or Jews or Negroes or Mexicans, the child is supplied with a ready-made target. And since Dad is the lawmaker and source of all wisdom in the kid's eyes, his prejudices are all too likely to seem natural and just.

It really isn't hard to teach a child tolerance, because kids have a tremendous sense of fair play and justice. Try dividing a slice of cake between two eagle-eyed youngsters and you'll see what I mean. (In our house, we figured out a brilliant solution to this: let one kid divide the cake and the other have first choice!) They also have a good deal of instinctive sympathy for other human beings—or even for animals. Many a time I've seen Diane's big eyes swim with tears over the wholly imaginary plight of some dog in a movie, or even a little dead sparrow in the street.

So, in a sense, you don't have to *teach* kids tolerance at all, because it's already there. Just try not to teach them intolerance. In other words, be tolerant yourself.

5. *Sweet Land of Liberty*

THE FIFTH ATTITUDE that we have tried to encourage in our kids is love of country. Not the boastful, swaggering, we-are-better-than-anybody brand of nationalism that sometimes passes for patriotism. But a kind of quiet pride and affection, pride that this country which is the strongest in the world is also the gentlest, and gratitude for the freedom and the unlimited opportunities that it offers.

There are many ways to encourage this kind of patriotism in kids. Stories about our great national heroes from Colonial or Revolutionary days. The pioneers who carved out the great empire of the West. The legendary figures of the Civil War. The blockade runners, the Indian fighters, the explorers who planted the American flag on the roof of the world, the lonely, persistent researchers in the laboratories, the great inventors. . . . Our country may still be young in terms of years, but no other nation has crowded so much history into so short a time.

Another way to make kids appreciate America is to give them some knowledge of other lands. Not many families can afford to travel abroad, perhaps, and until a kid is fourteen or fifteen I think foreign travel is largely wasted on him anyway. But it's possible to learn about conditions in other countries without actually going there, and the more a kid knows about worlds other than his own, the more likely he is to be glad he was born in the U.S.A.

I think it's likely that our kids—yours and mine—are going to have to face this problem of internationalism versus nationalism much more squarely than we have done. The world is shrinking rapidly, in terms of space and time. We are going to need a much higher degree of international cooperation, and to achieve that we are going to need much more understanding and good will.

I would like to see my own kids approach this problem with open minds, but also with a strong belief in the ideals and principles that made this country what it is today. I believe it is perfectly possible for a person to be strongly patriotic, and yet want to see the world more united than it is today. It may be visionary, but I can conceive of a planet where nations retain their identities and separate cultures, and yet live peaceably and harmoniously together.

Like all previous generations, my generation has made treaties and fought wars without achieving a lasting peace. Maybe our kids will do better.

6. *Laughter—Gift of the Gods*

THE SIXTH DESIRABLE ATTITUDE (you didn't think I'd forget *this* one, did you?) is humor. For over a quarter of a century, now, laughter has been my business—and I don't know of any better business, or any better medicine.

I think everyone is born with the seed of humor in him: babies smile almost before they do anything, and as far as I'm concerned it's *not* always gas pains! But how well the seed of humor grows depends on environment. Heaven knows, a laugh is a contagious thing. So if there's a lot of laughter in a house, if the parents like to tell jokes and amusing stories at the dinner table, if there's kidding and banter and good-humored teasing—then that seed of humor is going to grow.

And when it does grow, it's one of the most valuable attributes anybody can have. It brightens up every aspect of living. It lightens all sorts of loads. If you start almost anything—from a dinner party to some disagreeable chore—with a laugh, you've got a much better chance of making a success of it. Laughter puts things over—and that includes *you*. A person with a sense of humor is almost always popular and welcome anywhere.

It's a kind of international passport, too. Customs and manners vary enormously in different countries.

But humor doesn't. A husband-wife situation that brings a laugh in America will bring the same laugh in Russia or Japan.

Humor is a great equalizer—and a great teacher. It teaches a kid how to take a joke, even when the joke's on him. Some youngsters tend to be terribly sensitive to ridicule, or fancied ridicule. If they see that everybody in the family is laughed at occasionally, and that it's affectionate laughter, then they begin to relax and join in the fun.

I think kids should be taught that humor, to be valuable, must be kindly humor. I know some people whose wit leaves their victim stripped and helpless, with the feathered barb sticking right in his heart. This kind of savagery may get a momentary laugh, but it's not the kind of humor I want to pass along to my kids. It's really a form of disguised sadism.

I've noticed that humor is a pretty good barometer of how a person is feeling, of his basic state of mind. It tends to go into eclipse when people are worried or unhappy or upset. If it disappears altogether, this may be a real danger signal. It may mean that the person's problems are getting stronger than he is.

So expose your kids to humor. Laugh at their jokes, even when they're terrible. Don't shush them when *they* laugh, even if grandma is having her nap. The Bible says, "A merry heart doeth good like a medicine."

I think the Good Book is absolutely right!

7. *An Old-Fashioned Word*

THE SEVENTH AND LAST ATTITUDE is a blanket one, and it takes an old-fashioned word to describe it: *respect*. It's a big word, because it can include so much. Respect for work. Respect for achievement. Respect for learning. Respect for law. Respect for other people. Respect for self. Respect for the whole vast incomprehensible universe and its Creator. . . .

I can't tell you exactly how to pass on to your child this attitude of respect. In a way, it has to be the sum of everything you teach him. But I think, to begin with, he has to respect *you*. If he decides that you, his parent, are unfair, or dishonest, or lazy, it will be hard for him to acquire respect for justice, or honesty, or diligence. You are the first yardstick he has. He's going to measure the whole world by what he sees in you.

Next, I think it helps if you give him a few simple obligations when he's young, tasks that are well within his capabilities but that don't give him any selfish satisfaction. A kid who is taught to feed a dog or cat twice a day may not be making any tremendous sacrifice, but he is learning that there are hungers in the world other than his own. He's learning to respect the needs of other living creatures. The child who can be trusted to clean out a lovebird's cage regularly—as our Sharon can—will probably be trustworthy in far more important responsibilities later on.

I'm not trying to say that chores *necessarily* build character in kids. I think a lot depends on the spirit in which the chore is assigned. If it's made to seem like a punishment or a penalty, the kid is naturally going to resent it. If it's made to seem like a step toward adulthood, he'll probably be proud of it.

Another way to implant this attitude of respect in kids is to make them see how much human thought and endeavor and training go into certain things. Let them glance over a watchmaker's shoulder and see the infinite skill and patience with which he works. Take them to a factory and let them see the organization and efficiency that go into an assembly line. Invite an airline pilot or a doctor or a garage mechanic to your house for dinner and get them to talk to the kids about the challenge and fascination and intricacies of their particular specialties. It all adds up in building respect for skill, for knowledge, for other human beings.

Respect for the universe and its Creator is usually called reverence, and I think this can be implanted in children too. I believe most kids tend to follow the example of their parents in this area, and accept their beliefs—unless the early emphasis is too weak or too strong.

In my own childhood, I think the emphasis was too strong. Religion was all my foster father thought about or cared about. One of my earliest recollections is playing the triangle on street corners to attract a crowd so that my father could preach to the people. I was expected to go around with a tambourine and take up a free-will offering, too. To this day, I sometimes find myself looking at an audience and estimating how much they might contribute for a good sermon. Believe me, in those days it meant the difference between eating or not eating!

The result of all this was that my early feelings about religion were confused and somewhat resentful. It took me a long time to become aware of the importance religion can have in a person's life, and the good it does in the world.

When I was in college, religion was at a low ebb in this country. Now interest seems to be rising to a peak. Our Links have all been Sunday school goers—Sharon is particularly devoted, and I think Jack was president of his Sunday school class. To my way of thinking, Sunday school teachers have a wonderful opportunity to acquaint impressionable youngsters with moral and ethical values, unharrassed by either the home-mechanics of feeding, clothing, and washing that plague most mothers, or the school-necessities of readin', writin', and 'rithmetic that take up a schoolmarm's time. In many cases, they do a great job of implanting this attitude of respect that I'm talking about.

In the last analysis, I think, respect is a form of unselfishness, a recognition that there are values outside the individual that are just as important as his own ambitions and hopes and desires. If somewhere along the line you can get this concept implanted in your kid, you can just about stop worrying. Because what you have put there is the most important rule for living ever devised. It's the Golden Rule.

In Short . . .

So THERE ARE YOUR seven key attitudes: appreciation, curiosity, persistence, tolerance, patriotism, humor, and respect. Nobody, I suppose, ever gets a full quota of all of them. But parents can do a lot to make sure that their kids get a fair share.

A great psychiatrist, Dr. Karl Menninger, once said, "Attitudes are more important than facts."

So help your kid find the right attitudes. You'll be helping him win the battle of life.

Chapter 10
Kids Write the Darndest Things!

SOME DAY MY SON Robert will head up a spy ring, direct guerilla warfare, plot a revolution, or at the very least roister through a hitch in the Foreign Legion.

This premonition first came to me one day when I discovered a crumpled, hand-written note stuffed under his defunct ant farm. Judge for yourself:

> Plans for the Four Muskyteers. What we'll do to the Boys. Kick them. Sock them. Hold one boys arms and get a sirrender nowte or something. Take there books, jacket, and so on. Mabee take one prisiner and kill the rest. Have one Muskyteer sit on a bus in the middle of 2 people and do anything.
>
> What we'll do to the Girls. Can't think of anything bad enuff.
>
> P.S. Don't let the boys see this. If they get this, they might do the same to us.

Just what happened to the Four Muskyteers in the commission of this derring-do I'll never know, since it was part of the ultrasecret world of kids. And I never confessed that I knew anything, knowing that notes labeled "Private" were not for prying adult eyes. Robert was ten, then. He's a sophisticated teen-ager, now. I think it's time he knew I am a silent but sympathetic secret-sharer.

Then there was the night when Jack dropped a small, hand-written bombshell into the placid affairs of the Linkletter family. He was at about the same uninhibited age. I was at the studio doing "People Are Funny," and Lois was Captain of the Ship. Noting a sinister silence from Jack's room after the dinner bell had sounded, she opened the door to find, propped against his desk lamp, a note that carefully, gently, and sweetly drove her out of her mind:

> Dear Mom and Dad, I am going to take a little trip into the mountains. I am doing this to see what it is like. Don't be worried for I will not do anything dangerous. I will be with maybe ten other boys. Dad, you did once, so you won't be to mad. Mom, I know I have everything a boy wanted so if you want to know why I am going ask Dad. He can explain it better than I can.
>
> Love,
>
> Jack Linkletter (Link)
>
> P.S. Please don't be mad. Please, please, please. Don't report this to the police or anyone for it might get us in alought of trouble. Thank you. Love and kisses.

Well, I do know the end of *that* one. A distracted phone call from Lois and some frantic checking with other parents resulted in a hastily-assembled posse being dispatched into the rain-swept night. Headed by an experienced old frontiersman (me), the posse discovered Jack and one loyal henchman (the other eight had changed their minds) "camping" under a piece of water-logged canvas on the side of a canyon not far from his best pal's home.

So there were lectures and scoldings, but I must say that something in Dad was delighted by this display of adventuresome spirit, and to this day that farewell note of Jack's is one of my cherished souvenirs.

I guess parents have been saving their kids' childish scrawls ever since writing was invented. Here's one I came across that was written on a scrap of papyrus a couple of thousand years ago by a little boy in Egypt:

> Theon to his father Theon, greeting. It was a fine thing of you not to take me to town with you! If you won't take me to Alexandria, I won't write you a letter or speak to you or say goodbye to you . . . So send for me, I implore you. If you won't send, I won't eat, I won't drink, there now! Farewell.

Isn't it amazing how "alive" that letter is? You can almost see the frowning little boy trying to "manage" the father that he loves. And the father smiling, and tucking the note away in some safe place . . . so safe that it survived all these centuries. The boy and his father are long since dust, but their love for each other is still alive.

Or consider this one that arrived one day not long ago at the White House in Washington. My friend Jim Hagerty, the Presidential Press Secretary sent it to me:

> Dear Mr. President:
>
> It has come to my attention that when I graduate out of medical school there will probably be space travel with human beings. It has also come to my attention that a doctor (maybe a surgeon like I hope to be) will be needed on these flights, and many men will apply, and this is my application to be among those who will make the first flights. I am 11 years old and have done the following:
>
> I have given ants artifitial resperation, taken care of a toad that had been run over with a lawn mower, and know some human anatummy. Please consider my request.
>
> Thankfully,
Wayne Trebbin.

And Jim also sent me the reply that Wayne got from the Boss:

> Dear Wayne:
>
> Of course I shall see that your "application" to be a space flight surgeon will be carefully filed, but I rather suspect it would be a good idea for you to renew your suggestion at the appropriate time. None of us can quite visualize the world we will live in when you are a full-fledged doctor—say, in fifteen years from now.

In the meantime, I am fascinated by your medical knowledge and practice, and I wish you every success in your chosen career. You are very fortunate to know now exactly what you want to do with your life.

With my best wishes,
Sincerely,
Dwight D. Eisenhower.

At one point, on our House Party program, I asked viewers to send in samples of the darndest things their kids had written. The result was an epidemic of sprained backs among Los Angeles mail-carriers and a wave of total inefficiency in my office, where people sat around reading and laughing all day instead of doing any work. I can only offer you a tiny sampling of these masterpieces, but here are a few.

Schoolteachers, naturally, had the widest selection of gems from compositions, themes, excuses, and so on. Here's a somewhat puzzled nine-year-old writing a report on baby chickens:

> A baby chicken leads a very interesting life. It begins when the mother has the egg. It is a very hard sturrogle to come out of the egg. I'm not sure, but I think the Father has something to do with it. By that I mean I think the Father lays eggs too.

She must have been a city youngster. Like the kid I heard of who was visiting his country cousin and spotted some empty milk bottles in the grass. "Come quick, Johnny," he yelled. "I've found a cow's nest!"

One teacher sent me some interesting ideas that she

got from her third-graders when she asked for a one-paragraph essay on "How I Would Change History."

"At the beginning," wrote a young lady named Kathy Tyler, "I would make all the people without bones. Then they would be loose. Then we would crawl and things would be slow."

They sure would, Kathy!

In that same class, a young man named Stuart Shapiro had a more practical idea. "If I could change history," he wrote, "I would leave out the part that is taught in school."

Another viewer sent in the following "Little Boy's Essay on Anatomy," which I regard with a certain amount of suspicion because it is almost too good to be true:

> Your head is kind of round and hard and your brains are in it and your hair is on it. Your face is in front of your head where you eat and make faces. Your neck is what keeps your head out of your collar. It's hard to keep clean. Your shoulders are sort of shelfs where you hook suspenders on.
>
> Your stumick is something that if you do not eat often enough it hurts, and spinach don't help it none. Your spine is a long bone in your back that keeps you from folding up. Your back is always behind you no matter how quick you turn around. Your arms you have got to pitch with and so's you can reach the butter, and they keep your hands from falling off. Your fingers stick out of your hand so you can throw a curve and add up 'rithmetick. Your legs is what, if you have not got two of, you can't get

to first base. Your feet are what you run on, your
toes are what always get stubbed. And that's all
there is of you except what's inside, and I never
saw it.

Teachers are always getting excuse notes for one
thing or another. Here's one from a little boy who lost
his "absence" excuse and prepared his own:

Dear Teacher: Please excuse Buddy for being
absent yesterday. He was absent because he didn't
go to school.

And here's one handed in instead of the assigned homework:

Dear Teacher: I tried to do my arithmetic, but I
couldn't do some of them and I didn't have time to
do the ones I could do.

I also got a chuckle out of this one, addressed to a
teacher who had had to leave school because she was
pregnant:

Dear Teacher: We miss you. We are all fine. How
are you filling?

And then there was the kid who was designing a
safety poster warning his classmates not to play with
old lumber. This was his slogan: *It is dangerous to play
with old broads!*

If you don't think the love-bug bites early and hard
nowadays, cast your eye on this bashful communication
intercepted by a vigilant third-grade teacher:

Dear John,
Please exquse the paper please. If you would take

me to some secrut place do you know what Id do?
If you were coming near a bush where I was hiding
Id grab you pull you in—slang expreshun—and
KISS YOU.

Love,

Barbara.

P.S. How about going steady, PLEASE?

It looks as if the male of the species is getting more elusive than the female. Down in Memphis, Tennessee, when he received an ardent declaration of love from a young lady acquaintance, Allen Carson, age eight, sat down and wrote his admirer a firm note:

Dear Sally,
 I don't love you at all.

All my love,

Allen.

While out in Whittier, California, a young lady summed up her love life to date in the following poignant essay entitled "The Bravest Thing I Ever Did."

 I kissed a boy in fourth grade when he gave me
 a present and I didn't like him and I still don't.

And here's one from a mother whose stay in the hospital was lightened by a dispatch from the home front:

Dear Mommie,
 I am trying to be a good boy While you are gone.
I found grandpa's pipe and smoked it a little. It
didint taste good and it made me feel rite loneskome.
uncle henry said there was a looney tick loose in the
woods I think it aint so. we looked for it and oney

found some wood ticks How does a looney tick look?
we dont keep the house much clean Daddy said we
would clean it up before you came home. I didint
know if I should ask the Lord to make you better.
He might think I dont trust the doctor. Grandpa
said I could pray for the doctor. I wash my ears each
day I sent you love I wish you was home.

> Yours truly,
> Paul.

Professional writers say you should leave something
to the imagination of the reader. Here's an excerpt
from the letter of an eight-year-old who is already a
master. She's writing to her older sister who's away at
school:

Mother had a hard time today, she fell down and
tore her new stockings, then a mouse ran up her leg.
Daddy looked for it and couldn't find it. . . .

Then she added a couple of pages of household news,
and, as an afterthought:

P.S. The mouse ran down again.

Here's a cure for a cold from a young man who obviously can't spell "cathartic":

Go home, gargle your throat, take a good Catholic,
and go to bed.

I heard a good writer say once that the most effective way to write is just the way you talk, relaxed and
natural. Here's an exponent of that school, age eight,
writing to the parents of her best friend:

Dear Mrs. Corton and Mr. Corton,

I think Marion is getting to be an ofel bad girl and
you will never catch me playing with her again nor
talking with her again she said if my house got struck
with lightning I could not go over to her house and i
said if hers did she could not come over to my house
and she said she did not want to come over to my
house because it was to dirty and she taught me to
say O my god and I am going to pay her back because she has been ofel greedy with me for a long
time and i did not want to tell you on the 21 of August she slapped the baby just as hard as she could
because he wet his pants and I am just going to
give every body presents but marion. good-bye
from Jessie.

Kids are wonderfully casual when it comes to that
precious commodity, time. Here's a note a friend of
mine found on her return from a shopping trip:

Dear Mother,

I have gone fishing. What time shall I come home?
Love,
Leonard.

Another youngster left this invitation for his grandparents:

Dear Grandma and Grandpa,

Mom wants you to come to dinner tonight if you
get home before six.
Love,
Mike.

P.S. We are eating at four.

Disciplinary action on the part of parents sometimes

results in notes, penitent and otherwise. One six-year-old, sent to her room for being naughty, was told she couldn't come out until she agreed that she had been a bad girl. Half an hour later a "sirrender nowte" was pushed under the door:

> Dear Dadd,
>
> I am a stooput brat I hat myself from Bad Linda.

But sometimes mixed reactions show through. Here's a sample from a smoldering ten-year-old:

> Daddy. I don't know about liking you. If you keep after me I will hate you for sure. If you will stop getting after me I will love you better than I do now. From your half loving half hating girl to her half loving half hating Daddy.

Sometimes a line in a letter will be more revealing than the kid knows. Here's one from a twelve-year-old who had just returned to school:

> We got here in a hurry. The man who drove stopped on the road and drank two cans of oil.

Sometimes kids are more grateful for T.L.C. (Tender Loving Care) than we realize. Here's a note from an eight-year-old in Worcester, Massachusetts:

> Dear Mommy,
>
> I am very forchenard to have a mother who would want to get up two times at night to give me medissin. I know that you are very tired and I know that some night God forbid you should be sick I will get up to give you some medissin. I am very forchenard to have you and Daddy as parents. Because if you were

not my parents I might still be sick. All I can say is
thank you very much.

Love,
Ann

While out in Vernal, Utah, the guardians of the
law received this communication from a conscience-
stricken eight-year-old:

> Dear Poleece,
> I do not want to say this but I will. It is very bad
> news. I am a robber.

Here's an excerpt from an eleven-year-old's diary
that, needless to say, has stuck in my memory:

> Dear Diary:
> Well, another day is here. It is just like all days.
> I just sit rond doing nothing but watch TV. I
> watched Art Linklitter and then I got sick. Well I
> better go now.

And here are some dreams confided to his diary by a
nine-year-old:

> I would like to be father of two children and presi-
> dent of a bank. Because I like kids and banks. To be
> president of a bank you have to have a good record
> and no time in the pen. To be a father it's natural and
> easy.

Letters from camp would fill a book, and a pretty
funny book at that. Here are a few samples of un-
adorned camper's prose:

> Dear Mom and Dad,
> I'm not a bit homesick. Some of the kids are. The
> ones who have dogs. . . .

★

Dear Mom and Dad,

I have a big part in the camp play. It's about the Pied Piper. I am one of the rats. . . .

★

Dear Mother,

I am scribbling this note standing up because last night my bunk burned down. Nothing much happens here. . . .

★

Dear Dad,

I am having a good time. Can you please send me some city eggs? I don't like country eggs. . . .

Inevitably there are a few wistful souls who wish they were anywhere but in camp, although sometimes they make a valiant effort to conceal it. Here's a brave try:

Dear Mom and Dad,

I am not homesick. Please write to me. Are you coming Sunday? Please come. I need some clean towels. Write and tell me if you are coming. Please come and bring the baby. They keep us so busy here I don't have time to get homesick. Please come Sunday. Love, Paul.

P.S. Next year I think I'll come to camp for the shorter period.

Here's a young man who gets the same message across with fewer words:

Dear Mom,

There is a hundred and fifty boys in this camp. I wish it was a hundred and forty-nine. . . .

I think the one that tickled me most was this note

that the fond parents received from their eleven-year-old:

> Dear Mother and Daddy,
> Your worries are over. I am really growing up.
> I'm in a tend with older girls and all we talk about is
> boys and sex. Please send me a water pistol.
> Love,
> Linda

Here's a solicitous camper, thinking of other people's welfare:

> Dear Mom and Dad,
> Don't touch this postcard. I have poison ivy.
> Love . . .

How's this for social progress? It's a camp letter from a ten-year-old:

> Dear Mother,
> The first day here I didn't have HARDLY any
> friends. The second day I had a FEW friends. The
> third day I had FRIENDS and ENEMIES.
> Love,
> Anna.

And here's a resourceful young fellow:

> Dear Mom,
> I can't find my St. Christopher medal anywhere
> but do not worry. I have the St. Joseph's aspirin you
> put in my bag, so I will probably be okay.

The world can seem like an unfriendly place when you're only eight years old and away from home for the first time. This was eight-year-old Kathy's first communication from camp:

> Dear Mom,
> The foode is good, the camp is good, the wetter is good, the counseler is good, but—when you come to visit me, pleeze take me home—good.
> Love,
> Kathy

Little boys are made of sterner stuff—like this one:

> Dere Mom,
> Yesterday on a hike I almost stepped on a snake and that snake was six feet—and boy that's some tall snake!
> Love,
> Tommy

Here's true filial devotion for you:

> Hello Mom and Pop,
> They just told us that we cant eat until we write our parnts so I am just going to write enough this time to get something to eat.
> Love,
> Bud

So it goes, from the first of July every summer to the end of August. And sometimes even the camp authorities get into the act. Here's a note received by some friends of mine:

> Dear Friends,
> We are happy to be able to tell you, and we are sure that you will be proud to learn, that your son is now an Advanced Non-Swimmer.

No collection of kid letters would be complete without a couple addressed to that lovable old gentleman with the red suit and the white beard who lives at the North Pole. So here are a few:

Dear Santa,

I guess I have been half good and half bad most of this year, so you can just send me half of what I ask for . . .

★

Dear Santa,

Is it true that you don't come down chimneys any more? My Daddy says you come through a large hole in his pocketbook . . .

★

Dear Santa,

I am 6½ years old. 2 years ago I asked for a baby sister and I got it. Last year I asked for a baby brother to play with and I got it. So this year if its alright with mommy and daddy I would like to have a pony . . .

★

Dear Santa,

. . . and I want a washcloth for Granny's cat so he won't wear out his tongue . . .

★

Dear Santa,

. . . but what I'd like most of all, if your reindeer have any babies, would be to have a little baby reindeer for my own . . .

★

Dear Santa,

. . . and please could you bring Daddy some of whatever kind of hair tonic it is that you use. His head is beginning to come up through his hair . . .

★

Dear Santa,

. . . and please bring a bed for my daddy. I have a little bed, sister has a little bed, mommy has a bed, and poor daddy has no bed—he has to sleep with mommy.

The charm of the things kids write, like the appeal of the things kids say, lies in the combination of honesty and simplicity and unexpectedness. You can't imitate it, and you can't fake it. It comes from only one source: the mouths of babes.

One more, and then we'll move on. This one came in a note from a lady in Bristol, Connecticut:

Dear Art,

When my son had his sixth birthday, he received a new wallet. A couple of days later I found the identification card carefully filled out as follows:

Name—Charles

Age—6

Hair—Brown

Eyes—2.

Oh, it's a wonderful world, this secret world of kids. There are times when I wish I was back in it myself. But wishing won't make it so. Anyway, here's a thought I came across the other day that I like. I don't know who said it, but he was a wise man. Here it is:

"You're only young once . . . but that's enough if you work it right."

Chapter 11
Kids Around the World

"WHY IS IT," A FELLOW SAID TO ME the other day, "that here in the good old U.S.A., where we spend more thought and money on our kids than they do anywhere else on the planet, why is it that we also seem to have more trouble with them than they do anywhere else?"

He didn't wait for me to answer the question. He went right on: "Oh," he said, "I know there's a certain amount of rowdyism among certain elements in every country. But it seems to me that the less concern there is for young people, the better behavior patterns you get. Why is this?"

"Well," I started to say, but he was off and running again.

"By this time," he said, "most American parents are crammed with information about bringing up kids. They're loaded with child psychology. They've got Dr. Spock running out of their ears. They're experts on toilet training, motivation, sex education, and sibling rivalry. And what's the result? The result is that we seem to get more juvenile delinquency all the time, and every one of us knows at least half a dozen kids who are ill-mannered, obnoxious little brats. How do you explain that?"

"The explanation," I said, "probably lies . . ."

"I'll tell you what *I* think," he said, leaving me with my mouth still open. "I think a lot of our trouble stems from the fact that we let our kids grow up too fast. As a result, they run into a lot of problems, emotional and otherwise, that they're just not ready to handle. Don't you agree?"

"Well," I said feebly, "I. . . ."

"In other countries," he said, jabbing me with a firm forefinger, "the whole process is a lot slower. Babies are nursed longer. They go to school later. You don't see twelve-year-olds stumbling around on high heels like ridiculous little painted manikins. For simple economic reasons, courtship and marriage come later, with the result that . . ."

At this point, a majestic-looking matron sailed up and put a heavy hand on his shoulder. "Time we were going, Charles," she said. And off they went, leaving me so full of unexpressed ideas that I went right home and started a chapter called "Kids Around the World" —and this is it.

The Pattern Varies

LET'S START WITH A PARADOX. I'm convinced that, basically, kids are kids wherever you find them. Their fundamental reactions are the same in Siam and Siberia, Tripoli and Texas. I've watched their happy faces and heard them yelp with delight at dozens of circuses, puppet shows, and parties all over the world. Kids are kids are kids are kids . . . to paraphrase Gertrude Stein's similar observation about roses.

But their outward attitudes and behavior can be vastly different.

I found this out a while back when I thought I had a very bright idea. After a dozen years of interviewing American youngsters for radio and television, the notion occurred to me that on my trips abroad I ought to film the bright sayings of foreign children. Perhaps I could even get material for a sequel for my first "Kid" book and call it "Kids Say the Darndest Things All Over the World." It would, I told myself happily, be a natural!

But it wasn't. And for a surprising reason: most foreign children won't talk freely before adults. They won't say the unguarded and hilarious things that American kids blurt out without fear or favor. Their bright sayings stay right inside their little heads, a carefully guarded secret of the secret world of kids.

Sitting on a bench under the Atomium of the Brussel's World Fair with a curly-headed Belgian boy, I began my adventures with kids around the world. After some routine questions designed to put him at ease, I asked him one that almost never misses: "What's the funniest thing you've ever seen?"

He thought for a moment, then soberly replied, "Clowns are quite funny."

"That's true," I agreed. "But how about something that happens at your house? Maybe something funny about your mother or daddy?"

"Oh," he gulped uncertainly, looking quite shocked, "I don't know of anything like that!"

Now, that same question in America might have brought out an answer like this (in fact, it did): "The funniest thing I ever saw was the time Mommy forgot to fix a button and when she dived into the pool at our neighbor's house, her suit came off!"

The American youngster thought this was funny—
and I do too. But the little Belgian boy would have
been shocked, horrified, abashed, and aghast.

This reverential attitude where parents are concerned isn't limited to Europe. In the beautiful ceremonial gardens of a palace in Kyoto, Japan, I asked
a little doll-like Japanese girl, "Do you have any
family rules?"

"Always obey your father," she murmured.

"And how would you change your father if you
could?" I asked her cheerily.

"Change my father?" She looked absolutely bewildered: such a thought was beyond her, unthinkable.
She had no answer.

Here in America a seven-year-old answered the
question casually with: "I'd make my daddy like to
watch Zorro on TV instead of those messy wrestlers."

On another occasion, riding down the Seine on a
"bateau mouche" river boat, my cameras were trained
on a delightful French child of seven who answered my
question about table manners by saying, primly, "We
must always eat our vegetables."

In America, the month before, a freckle-faced tom-
boy had replied with a grin, "We aren't allowed in our
house to spit on the floor!" She was just having fun at
my expense.

And so it went. In Berlin, Stockholm, Hong Kong,
and Athens, I ran into the same problem: the kids re-
fused to come out of their shell. They had been trained

to be polite, quiet and, above all, careful around grownups. They weren't going to risk any opinions in front of this strange American and his cameras because they knew children were to be seen and not heard when "out in company."

This, for better or worse, is not the American pattern. So let's take a look at the chief differences in the "bringing up" of a child abroad as compared with what goes on here. Maybe we can evaluate what is good and what is not so good in both systems.

Our Civilization on Wheels

NOT LONG AGO I read a statement by a somewhat disgruntled psychiatrist to the effect that

American parents have lost a knowledge which all other creatures on this earth possess: namely, how to raise their young."

With this statement I heartily disagree. Americans have not lost any such thing. It's true that we raise children differently from parents in most other places, and it's also true that we allow or even encourage a degree of freedom of action and expression generally frowned upon elsewhere. But our system is not wholly bad, as I intend to show.

When you compare American kids with the children of, say, some European nation, you have got to realize that the U.S.A. differs radically from any other nation under the sun, and some of these differences are bound to show up in the way kids are handled. America is a restless, dynamic, ever-changing, semi-pioneer country. More families move to new homes in new neighborhoods or new cities than in any other country under the sun. This one fact alone has changed patterns of life and created perplexing problems never before faced by parents anywhere in the world.

The chief result, I think, is a kind of rootlessness that children feel keenly. A familiar background, a sense of belonging, these are steadying factors in time of stress. In Europe, it's not unusual to find families that have lived in the same neighborhood—or even the same house—for ten generations. Everyone knows everyone else. There is a protective feeling throughout the community toward all the kids of the community.

Each family tends to have its accepted place in the civic scheme of things, so that the well-known American rat-race to be better, richer, or more popular than your next-door neighbor doesn't develop so fast or so furiously.

In our country, many a family hardly has time to get acquainted with the folks next door before the breadwinner is shifted to another plant in another city, and the whole pathetic process of trying to put down roots has to begin all over again.

So, in lots of places, lots of American kids are always "outsiders." Like little lost animals, they go sniffing around a new neighborhood looking for acceptance. Sometimes they get it. Sometimes not. Opportunities for getting into trouble multiply, because few families know much about the "new kid," and feel no responsibility for him.

In Copenhagen, last year, I saw a red-faced matron carrying a wriggling little demon down the street almost five blocks to where his mother was waiting to get a first-hand report of his rascality—which happened to be stealing apples. Not a very grave crime, but the point is, he hadn't a chance to get away with it and then go on to wonder what else he could steal. He was being protected, actually, by an invisible network of neighborhood "togetherness."

Another great difference between American and European ways of life can be seen in the role that the father plays. In America, countless irreverent jokes center about "dear old Dad." On innumerable television tubes, he is pictured as the bumbling, well-meaning, henpecked dope who can't fix a sticky door, wash dishes without breaking Ma's favorite plate, diaper the baby without getting the pin in his own thumb, or answer the doorbell without buying every idiotic gadget some fast-talking salesman has to offer.

In short, the image of Father in the U.S.A. has become a blurred and wishy-washy one, tyrannized by the boss, victimized by Mom, and kidded by the kids. And while it may not be a wholly accurate image, it has proved real enough to be frightening to family counselors everywhere. Stout defenders of "Pop" are now arising on every hand and are prodding him to pick up the family sceptre and assert his authority as of yore. But the consensus is that he has a long way to go.

Meantime, in most other countries of the world, Father's word is law. At the dinner table, he directs the conversation. In times of family stress, Dad is the one who gives the orders that are to be followed unquestioningly. He controls the purse strings with iron fingers. He punishes with hand, stick, or strap (in general, there's less nagging for small crimes, harsher punishments for big ones). Dad is the final authority about where the family goes, what it does, how it lives, everything.

This clearly defined authority gives a growing child a sense of security and peace of mind—unless it's administered so harshly that it leads to resentment. Kids abroad seldom try to play that favorite American game in which Dad and Mother are divided and then conquered. They can't do this because even Mom has to get permission for most things from Dad.

In America, women have achieved freedom and equality with men in just about every direction. Today a third of our labor force is female, and we see working mothers and wives in every imaginable kind of job. This has increased the family income, all right, but it has brought about some very real troubles inside the American family circle.

When Junior comes home from school at three o'clock, and the house is empty, he looks for something to do. What he finds to do may be good, or it may be bad, but his parents won't know about it until they get home from work. In some families, of course, there's Grandmother, or Auntie, or even hired help to hold the fort. But such substitutes rarely represent the kind of authority the kid needs in his restless, growing years.

In other parts of the world, women don't have the job opportunities that exist here. Mom is much more likely to be home dishing up the stew than out chasing the extra paycheck to keep up with the installments on the care she needs to earn the paycheck. So mothers tend to be in the home, where their children need them.

I think it's hard to over-state the importance of this. In the past decade, in the larger cities throughout the world, wherever women begin to play an important part in industry, the creeping blight of juvenile delinquency begins to appear. In London the "Teddy boys"— young hoodlums who affect Edwardian clothes and haircuts—are a growing menace. In Paris, Rome, and Berlin their counterparts are being talked about. With more and more metropolitan families trying to make ends meet by having both parents work, the problems that afflict American families are beginning to appear all over the world.

The Menace of the Broken Home

WHAT I'M SAYING, of course, has been said many times: to develop properly, kids need the kind of love and security that can be found only inside a stable, happy home. In countries overseas, partly because of Mother's economic dependence on her man, partly because of stricter religious rules, the divorce rate is much lower than it is in the United States. In India, until recently, divorce was almost unheard of, and in predominantly Catholic countries all over the world it has been held to a minimum.

Here in America, unfortunately, we have the highest divorce rate in the world. In California, where I live, one out of every four marriages ends in divorce. Among the very young people of seventeen to twenty who are rushing to the altar, the rate is even higher.

This is bad enough where there are no children. But where kids are involved, divorce almost always results in frustration, divided loyalties, and bitterness . . . sometimes in actual neglect. Where Mother gets custody of the children, they lack the strong guiding hand of a father. When Dad occasionally gets the youngsters, he is all too likely to over-compensate for their lack of a mother by spoiling them. The bewildered kids can scarcely be blamed if they turn their bitterness against other children, their parents, or even themselves.

Do I think that discipline tends to be too lax in many American families? Yes, I do. Visiting some Swiss friends of mine recently in Geneva, I commented on how well behaved their four children were. They kept in the background, letting the older people talk. They waited until everyone had been served before asking for sweets. When bedtime arrived, and they were told quietly to go, they vanished without an argument.

When I complimented my host, and asked for his secret formula, he smiled and said, "We expect them to behave . . . so they do!"

This brings up a question that we might well ask ourselves here in the U.S.A.: "Do we really expect our kids to behave?" I doubt it. In far too many American homes there's a good deal of loose kidding about how Junior is the terror of the neighborhood. And indulgent smiles appear when some one tells how one of the kids got away with murder recently by staying out for the second movie without telling anyone where he went. It's almost as if the parent were saying, "See what a good sport I am, how tolerant, how understanding, how kind!"

There are times when I think we Americans carry this business of being a good sport too far. The phrase has come to be a sort of magic talisman in relations between people and involves all sorts of vague values ranging from being a good loser at tennis to shrugging off disastrous pranks committed by the kids of the family.

This phony business of wanting to be considered "a good sport" is based on a desperate yearning to be liked by everyone, especially your own kids. So in some families, no matter what happens to the house, the furniture, the car, or the neighbors' property, the parent will summon up a glassy grin and mutter, "Kids will be kids."

How many times has every parent heard his offspring beg: "Aw, c'mon, be a good sport, let me stay out till just two o'clock!" If this gambit fails, then the kid will remind Dad that he was a kid once himself. And so forth, and so on.

And it's amazing how many grownups fall for this sort of guff. Perhaps in a guilty desire to compensate for the hours they've skipped with their children, or in a sentimental rush of childhood memories, they lower the bars and away goes the youngster into a situation that everyone knows spells trouble.

In Madrid, a year ago, I asked a father if he ever thought about being a "good sport" in his dealings with his children. He snorted: "Senor, in my country it is the children who must be good sports. We tell them what they can do, where they can go, and when to come home—and if they don't, we have a good sport here in Spain called *pantalones encendidos* or roughly translated, "the seat of the pants are aflame."

As I have said before in this book, the best sports I know among parents are those who spend time with their kids and teach them by example the rules of the game of life. This takes more patience, skill, and guts than any other kind of contest that I know. To rein in your own errant impulses, guard your language, and do the right thing at the right time under the clear-eyed scrutiny of your own kids is the toughest test of character and spiritual stamina yet devised.

Country Clubs vs. Colleges

ANOTHER WAY we Americans differ sharply from other countries is in the way we handle the problem of education. Our school methods and theories amaze and sometimes appall educators from other lands.

A dozen years ago, when I first began to interview children on the air, now and then I would meet a boy or girl who had recently moved to this country from somewhere abroad. I'd ask them how they liked American schools.

"Fine!" they would say with enthusiasm. "The schools in America are lots better."

"Why?"

"Because they're so much more fun. We don't have to work so hard. Besides, we've already studied most of the courses they're giving us."

I got this answer so often that I finally stopped asking the question. I felt too embarrassed for our American schools.

The truth is, education is a serious matter abroad. It's not taken for granted the way it is here. Children attend school for longer hours, take home more work to be finished, and have less extra-curricular activities. They are disciplined and regimented right down to the school uniform, which is a common sight in any European town when school lets out. Kids come marching down the street two by two, looking as if they'd all come out of the same mold. And while there's the romping and fun you'd expect to find among children everywhere, there is also a seriousness of purpose where school is concerned that you don't generally find in the United States.

Overseas, getting good grades and passing your subjects successfully is a matter of family honor. When a kid does badly in school, the pride of the whole family is in jeopardy, and woe to the delinquent student if he doesn't haul up his wavering marks.

Of course, it's easier to make a twelve-year-old do his homework if there's no "Gunsmoke" to watch, or no TV set in the house at all. And seventeen-year-old Hans is much more likely to be wrestling with Latin if the gang is not beeping the old jalopy's horn outside the window. Hans is lucky if he owns a bicycle.

In most other countries, if the family intends to send the children to a university, then the midnight oil is really burning seven nights a week. Being a professional man is the dream of every ambitious boy all over the world, and in most places the gulf between the low-paid life of a working man and the relative affluence of a professional man can only be bridged by a college education.

Here in the United States, the average high school kid confidently expects to go on to college. He may not know what he's going to study, or what he wants to be, but he knows very well how much fun fraternity life is and what a kick he's going to get out of football week-ends. He's not sure whether he'll ever graduate, because studies may get tough. But in the meantime there will be dances and bonfire rallies, and somewhere along the line boy will meet girl, boy will romance girl, and they'll live happily on something, somewhere, forever after.

If I sound a little exasperated about all this, it's probably because I had to fight and work for my own college degree, and it annoys me to see so many youngsters take their opportunities for granted and then just throw them away. And I'm not the only one who feels this way. Recently I read an article by Jerome Ellison, a member of the faculty at Indiana University, in which he said flatly that a preposterous number of girls go to college simply to get married and an equally preposterous number of boys are there simply to have a good time. They have no interest in learning anything that requires discipline or effort. They avoid foreign languages and shun mathematics like the plague.

In his article, Ellison invited anyone who doubts this to take his place some morning on the lecture platform. "Let him face an early class he's knocked his brains out to prepare for. Let him address the blank stares and vacant faces of a roomful of students who knocked their brains out the night before at the Sophomore Twitch, the Winter Willies, the Monumental Maul, the Greek Tweak, or in short, at goofing off."

Families in other countries just can't afford such nonsense. (Neither can we, really.) Long hours are spent debating Junior's chances of making the big upward leap in earning power and in society. And anxious months are consumed in worries over finances, as Papa scrimps and saves to make college for Junior possible.

Overseas, if fifty out of a thousand high school students get into college, they're fortunate. And those fifty had better be prepared for stiff entrance examinations after having passed all their lower grade subjects with high marks. In France, until very recently, two examinations were required for college entrance. A written and an oral test were given each applicant, and these really put him through the wringer. So many complaints were received, and so many first-class students were turned down, that not long ago the oral exams were repealed—over the wails of the educators.

Once a foreign student gets into college, there's no such folderol as campus secret societies, or hazing, or football rallies, or constant social events. Instead, you get serious discussions about international affairs, or labor problems, or the competition between generations and its social consequences. Debates, fierce political rallies, and intense young people concerned with the future of world affairs are more to be seen than sporty get-togethers around country clubs or frat houses for the purpose of verifying the vital statistics of the reigning campus queen.

In other words, educational values are different abroad than they are here, and generally speaking the result is a better educated young person.

The Case for the American System

BY NOW YOU probably think that I am going overboard in favor of alien customs when it comes to raising kids. Actually, I'm not. When it comes to polite, self-effacing kids who take their education seriously, I do think some other countries have an edge on us. But I also think that our American schools and homes tend to produce a kid who is more daring, imaginative, resourceful, independent, and perhaps in the long run happier.

For one thing, the American kid has far more opportunities to investigate life and to express himself than his foreign counterpart. Most American youngsters can swim, shoot, skate, ski, ride, play tennis, golf, or just about any game you care to name. As a result, they're bigger and stronger than kids elsewhere, and they have more confidence.

Since they're less regimented, in school and in the home, they are more individualistic. It would be hard to introduce the goose-step mentality into this country. Time after time, during the last two wars, it was demonstrated that our opponents were excellent soldiers so long as they could fight by the book. But whenever the situation became fluid, and it was every man for himself, the American citizen-soldier made a monkey out of his enemy. He knew how to think and act for himself.

American kids are more versatile because they have far more things to play with, take apart, and reassemble. In other countries, kids have few if any possessions. I remember one time giving a bicycle to one of the war orphans we adopted. He simply could not believe that it was his, to keep. He thought it was just a loan that he would have to give back to us when we left. This made quite an impression on me. In our house, Jack could have two aqua-lungs (and did); Robert could earn enough money to buy hi-fi equipment, or a beat-up jalopy to conduct a mechanical post-mortem on. So my kids knew about these things. The foreign child couldn't know because he might as well have wished for the moon.

I said that Robert could earn money. Here again, the American kid has a tremendous advantage. In this country, if a youngster wants to earn some cash in his summer vacation, he can usually find a job. Last year, in Rome, I tried to find some spare-time work for my Foster Plan child, Alberto Di Raco. Alberto is seventeen, a fine, intelligent, ambitious lad. He wanted to earn some money during the summer and after school to help with his college plans. I was dismayed to find out that in Italy this was an utter impossibility. Businessmen and government officials to whom I brought the problem looked at me in disbelief. Surely, they said, I knew that for a man with no profession there was only the most menial kind of work, with long hours and low wages. I finally gave up after a series of phone calls that even included my friend James Zellerbach, our Ambassador in Rome.

Kids abroad live under certain invisible restrictions, too. There's a tendency in "old" countries to think that the status quo is inevitable and unchangeable. "What was good enough for my father is good enough for me, and should be good enough for you." American kids

reject this philosophy. They think they can be anything they please. So they're likely to have more drive,
more resilience, more energy, more bounce.

In Short . . .

SO THERE YOU HAVE IT. I think we could
learn something from our friends across the sea when
it comes to good manners and respect for learning. But
I think our system, with all its faults, does produce the
type of kid who is eager and extroverted, who can roll
with the punches, who is quick on his feet, and who will
come up with a remarkable number of ideas that fit our
kind of civilization.

Your American youngster may know less Latin and,
be hazy about higher mathematics and get lost in the
maze of philosophy. But he has the toughness of mind
and the capability for compromise and the ability to
get along with people that enable him to swim, not sink,
in our highly competitive capitalistic society.

I always liked the story of the brilliant student who
helped coach a rough and ready football player
through his college requirements in math. Years later,
the two met. The scholar was now making $6,500 a year
teaching arithmetic at a high school. The ex-athlete
was making $250,000 a year manufacturing key rings.

After the first greeting, the teacher inquired curiously as to how the tycoon figured out his profit and loss statements.

"Oh," said the former tackle, "it's easy. We make the gimmicks for $1.00 and sell them for $5.00. I know that's only a five per cent profit, but somehow I knock off a quarter million a year!"

Chapter 12

Kids STILL *Say the Darndest Things!*

ONE FINE DAY, in the spring of 1957, I received a letter from a gentleman, then unknown to me, who worked for a New York publishing house. His name was Bernard Geis, and he said that his health was being endangered by a habit his wife had developed of waking up in the middle of the night and laughing right in his ear. When asked for the cause of all this merriment, Mrs. Geis would chuckle about a television program called "Art Linkletter's House Party" and the remarkable things that were said by the child guests who appeared on it. "You ought to watch it," Mrs. Geis told her husband. "Those kids say the darndest things."

In his letter to me, Mr. Geis reported that he had watched it and, being a man who thought in terms of books, he was wondering if it might not be both pleasant and profitable to put some of these remarkable remarks in publishable form. It would, said Mr. Geis firmly, undoubtedly be a best seller. So how about it?

The odd thing about this was that for a long time I had been thinking of writing a book about my interviews with kids and had just been putting it off. Now, thanks to Mrs. Geis's midnight mirth and Mr. Geis's consequent insomnia, there was no excuse for putting it off any longer. So we assembled a slender volume written by Linkletter, edited by Geis, titled by Mrs. Geis, illustrated by Charles M. Schulz, foreworded by a fellow named Walt Disney, and published by Prentice-Hall.

We offered it to the unsuspecting public in late October—with remarkable results. Although the book didn't appear until the last quarter of the year, it became the best selling non-fiction book of 1957, racking up sales of 180,000 copies in less than three months. In 1958 it also led the non-fiction parade with a total sale, by that year's end, of over 450,000 copies. Pocket Books then brought out a paper-back edition in the spring of 1959, and in September the president of that firm, Leon Shimkin, presented me with a golden kangaroo, symbolic of two million copies sold.

So Mr. Geis's prediction of a best seller came resoundingly true, and the pair of us wound up not only as friends but as business associates.

It's not really immodest of me to report all this because most of the credit for the phenomenal success of *Kids Say the Darndest Things!* goes to the kids themselves. They supplied the humor in the form of unrehearsed quips, slips and shockers. All I had to do was incite them to make their priceless remarks and then set them down on paper.

I'm glad to report that they're still supplying those ingredients, five days a week, on our House Party program. When I stand up there before twelve million viewers and ask a question, I still have to hold onto my hat, hair, teeth, and sanity, because I never know what sort of verbal fast-ball, curve, or slider I'm going to get back.

The other day, for example, I asked one of my four small visitors what her favorite story was.

"*The Three Little Pigs,*" she replied.

"Which little pig do you like best," I asked innocently.

"The one," she said promptly, "that wee-wee'd on the way home!"

When the laughter died down, I decided I might as well go on and run the whole gantlet. "What's your favorite story?" I asked the next five-year-old.

"*Jack Be Nimble.*"

This sounded like a safe and sane choice. "What does that story teach you?" I asked.

"Don't jump over a candlestick in your night-gown or you might burn something important."

I moved on hastily to my third guest. Same question.

"My favorite story," she said shyly, "is *Snow White*

and the Seven Orfs."

"What does it teach you?"

"That you're happy if you have seven men in the house who whistle while you work."

The last one was the crusher. This young man said his favorite tale was *The Three Bears.*

"What does it teach you?" I wanted to know.

"Lock your door when you go out or else you're likely to find a girl in your bed!"

At one point on the House Party program I offered to give an autographed copy of the book to any viewer who would send in a kid's saying bright enough or funny enough to be used on the air. The result was a flood of mail that is still coming in. Here, highly condensed, are just a few of these gems:

Five year old: "I've got the smartest dog. All I have to say is 'Are you coming in or aren't you?' and he either comes in or he doesn't."

Three-year-old, sadly, on being told she had her shoes on the wrong feet: "But, Mommy, these are the only feet I have."

Six-year-old, hopefully, on being told there would be no school because of George Washington's birthday: "Can I go to George's party?"

☆

Five-year-old, on being given her allowance: "Oh, I just *love* to hold this money; it makes my hand feel so good!"

☆

First-grader, on being told that if he wanted to go to the washroom he was to hold up two fingers: "How's *that* going to help?"

☆

Four-year-old in church for the first time, as the usher approaches with collection plate: "Don't pay for me, Daddy. I'm under five."

☆

Seven-year-old breathlessly describing a wedding: "The bride had a beautiful white dress, and the pallbearers wore white too!"

☆

Wide-eyed little boy in a restaurant; his mother has just asked the waiter for the left-over steak to take home to the dog: "Oh, boy! At last! We're gonna get a dog!"

☆

Dialogue between mother and five-year-old who's in the next room:
   "Mommy, can I eat this candy I found on the floor?"
   "No, there are germs on it."
   Slight pause.

"Mommy, can I eat it now? I licked all the germs off."

☆

Four-year-old, bursting into tears at the dinner table: "My teeth just stepped on my tongue!"

Actually, a lot of funny remarks originate at the dinner table. Here's a three-year-old giving her reaction to Thanksgiving Dinner. "I didn't like the turkey, but I liked the bread the bird ate." And a four-year-old, holding out her well-gnawed corncob: "Please may I have some more beans on my stick?" It was a four-year-old, too, trying hard to explain that she wanted a boiled egg for breakfast, who said: "I want it left shut."

Sometimes it isn't so much what kids say as the way they say it. In a Brooklyn school not long ago a first grader named Ricky complained of having a stomach ache, so the teacher sent him to the principal. When he returned, he was walking in a most extraordinarily sway-backed fashion. Naturally, the teacher wanted to know why he was behaving in such a peculiar way.

"Well, said Ricky, "I told the principal I had a stomach ache, and he said he'd drive me home if I could stick it out till noon."

☆

Overheard dialogue between two six-year olds:
"Our TV is busted. The man is coming to fix it."

"How will he do that?"

"Oh, he'll probably open it up and take out all the dead cowboys."

☆

And a revealing conversation piece between two little girls, one showing the other around her house.

"This is Daddy's den. Does *your* daddy have a den?"

"Oh, no. He just growls all over the house."

☆

Here's another thumbnail sketch of dear old Pop:

First small boy: "Say, have you ever heard of the Devil?"

Second s.b.: "Oh, it's the same old story as the one about Santa Claus. It's nobody only Dad."

☆

Some viewers manage to paint a vivid portrait in just a line or two.

Dear Art,
    I wish you could have seen our three-year-old this morning, in full cowboy regalia, sneaking up on a flock of robins, whipping out his gun, and snarling, "Put up your legs, birds!"

Here's another that had the magic quality of making me "see" it happening:

Dear Art,
    My two-year-old, George, was playing in the yard when a cat came strolling by. He started to pet it, so

I called out, "George, that cat doesn't know you. He might scratch you." He bent over, looked the cat straight in the eye and said, "Cat, I'm George Black-well."

Which reminds me of the mother who looked out and saw her little girl with her hand up to the elbow in the mouth of a large, strange, unfriendly-looking dog. "Linda!" she shrieked. "Take your hand out of that dog's mouth!"

"It's all right, Mommie," said Linda reassuringly. "I just washed my hands. They're clean."

Speaking of dogs, here's a note that a lady in St. Augustine took the trouble to write me last December. Matter of fact, she wrote it on Christmas Day:

> Dear Art,
> You might enjoy this story about my little four-year-old nephew. He wanted a dog for his birthday, but we thought he was too young for a real dog, so we gave him a calico dog instead. He took one look at it and burst into tears.
> "What's the matter?" we asked. "Don't you like your little doggie?"
> "No," he cried. "I want a dog that's made of dog!"

A lot of people worry about the effect of TV on kids, and my own opinion, as I've said before, is that a lot of kids get too much of it. But here's a note from the mother of a young man who seems destined to wind up as a television *writer:*

Dear Art,

I had told bed-time stories until I was blue in the face. Still my wide-awake five-year-old begged for more. So, hoping to save my vocal cords, I suggested that he tell me a story.

He proceeded to make up one about three little kittens deep in darkest Africa, happily hemming them in with such perils as crocodiles, cannibals, and a couple of creatures from outer space.

Personally, I didn't see any way out for the poor little kittens, and evidently Gary was pretty well stumped, too. After a few minutes I asked, "Well, then what happened?"

More silence and troubled thought. But finally, brightening, my son concluded his narrative:

"Then," he beamed, "God *swooped* down with a *Winchester* . . ."

Kids seem so sophisticated nowadays that sometimes it startles you to find out how innocent they really are. The mother of one of my four-year-old friends was toweling him after his bath when suddenly he announced that he had discovered how to tell girls from boys.

"Have you?" asked his mother resignedly. "How?"

"By their haircuts," said Junior happily.

Another mother overheard two little five-year-old girls discussing the arrival of a new baby next door. "You know," said one, "Mrs. Brown said she knew right away that she had a baby girl. How do you suppose she knew that?"

"Oh, it's easy," said the other. "You just press a new baby on the top of the head, and if it's soft, it's a girl!"

Then there was the mother in Massachusetts who overheard her little girl, age nine, being entertained by a neighbor's son, age seven. Roger was telling Alice how he and his family had come across a nudist colony while on a country walk.

"Were they men or women?" asked Alice eagerly.

"I don't know," said Roger. "They didn't have clothes on."

Kids have their problems, all right, but living in their secret world they're not too much troubled by some of the things that plague us adults. The other day on House Party I asked a seven-year-old if it worried her when she heard the words "fall out."

"Not much," she said. "Two of mine are loose and one has fallen out, but I don't care."

Here's a mother reporting an unforgettable moment in her life:

> One hot summer day I decided to take a shower while my children were out playing. I left the bath-

room door open. Unknown to me, my five-year-old
son chose this moment to show off our new house to
some friends. As I turned off the water and pulled
back the shower curtain, my son said politely: "And
this is my mother!"

One reason, I'm sure, that kids are often baffled by
grownups is that grownups are always issuing orders
that seem to violate the strict childhood rules of logic.
One little boy, being instructed to squeeze the tooth-
paste tube from the bottom, said bewilderedly, "But,
Mother, there's none left in that end." A little girl,
being urged to button her dress, replied: "How can I
button it when the buttons are in back and I'm in
front?"

Then there was the first-grader in Knoxville who was
asked by her grandmother if she knew how to spell the
word "up." She answered quickly, "Yes, u-p." Then
she was asked to spell the word "down." Not having
had this word, she hesitated for a moment. Then logic
came to her rescue. "That's easy," she said. "U-p spells
up. P-u spells down!"

Well, why not?

Sometimes the freshness with which a child looks at
things can make you stop and think. A friend of mine,
carrying his three-year-old into a dark room, felt her
arms tighten around his neck. "Turn off the dark,
Daddy," she whispered. Not "turn on the light," but
"turn off the dark." A pretty good phrase to live by.

A first-grader I heard of offered a pretty sharp

commentary on our way of life when her mother warned her to be careful crossing the streets on her way to school. "Don't worry, Mummy," she said reassuringly. "I always wait for an empty space to come by."

And it was a three-year-old, watching another little girl cross the street alone, who said indignantly, "Look, Mama, that little girl is crossing the street herself, and she doesn't even have a mother in her hand."

It's always fun when David slays Goliath, when the office worm finally turns and bites the boss, or when a kid gently but firmly puts an adult in his place. One North Carolina youngster was saying his go-to-bed prayers in a very low voice.

"I can't hear you, dear," his mother said finally.

"Wasn't talking to you," said Billy crisply.

While down in Clearwater, Florida, a small fry who had just pledged allegiance to the flag was asked if he knew what "liberty and justice for all" meant. He shook his head. "Justice means being fair," the teacher said. "Liberty means that you're free."

"Well," said her pupil indignantly, "I'm certainly not free. I'm five-and-a-half, and you know it."

I could go on indefinitely with these stories sent in by viewers—for which I hereby tender thanks—but let's get back to the kids on House Party. In case you've never seen the program (horrid thought) let me explain that we draw most of our small guests from the Los Angeles Public School system, where they are selected by their teachers or principals. When school is out, we recruit kids from summer school, from the YMCA or the YWCA, from the Boy or Girl Scout organizations, and so on.

Before each show, I talk briefly with our small visitors, try to put them at ease or "warm them up" as we say in show business. But I never try to tell them what to say. For one thing, the whole show would instantly become stilted and artificial. For another, I couldn't think of anything half as funny or as startling as the things they're going to say under their own steam.

Visualize me, then, easing my 200 pounds onto the edge of the small platform and getting down—literally —on the level of my four bright-eyed associates (I almost said "victims," but a lot of the time I'm not sure who's victimizing whom!). I'm armed with a few standard questions designed to unlock family closets and rattle the skeletons therein. But I don't have any hard-and-fast rules, or cut-and-dried techniques. I just take a firm grip on the microphone, look my small friend in the eye, take a deep breath, and start asking questions. It's just as easy as rolling off a log—except that the log sometimes turns out to be forty feet from the ground!

Maybe on one show I'll decide to probe for deep moral values and I'll come up with gems like these:

From an eleven-year-old: "If at first you don't succeed, the heck with it!"

☆

From a nine-year-old: "Do unto others before they do it to you!"

☆

Definition of a "good sport," from an eight-year-old: "After you knock a guy down, help him up—unless he's bigger than you."

Another day I'll ask a simple question: "What sort of animal would you like to be?" And get answers like these:

☆

"A duck."
"Why?"
"Because I've never been one."

☆

"A fly."
"Why?"
"Because then I'd get to go on all the picnics."

☆

"A horse."
"Why?"
"Because you can run and eat hay and you don't have to raise your hand when you have to go to the bathroom."

Kids often turn out to be great story-tellers, and they don't waste any words. Here are some short-shorts:

270

☆

What can your dad do around the house?
—Well, once he tried to fix the car.

☆

What happened?
—We had to get a new car.

☆

What do you want to be when you grow up?
—An airline hostess.

☆

Why?

—Because my aunt was one and she told me you can marry rich millionaires.

☆

Who'd your aunt marry?
—The janitor at the airport.

☆

What do you want to be?
—A fireman.

☆

Why pick that?
—Because my dad says I'm dumb enough to be one.

☆

What does your dad do?
—He's a fireman.

I think the main reason we've had so much luck with this particular part of our House Party program is that you get enormous variety packed into a very few minutes on the air. And we never run out of material, because we're dealing with human nature itself. Notice how a kid can paint a delightfully cockeyed picture in a single sentence:

☆

What makes your mother the maddest?
—When my dad comes home, takes off his shoes, opens a bottle of beer, sits down in front of the TV set and whistles at all the pretty girls on the program.

☆

What's the funniest thing you've seen this summer?
—Dad came home, hit Mom on the back of her lap with a chair, and she threw a cherry pie at him.

☆

What does your dad do for fun?
—He chases cats.

What does your mother do for fun?
—She puts ice-cubes in my father's beer while he's out chasing cats.

☆

What does your dad do?
—He's a doctor and gives shots.

What does he do for fun?
—He sees if ladies are going to have babies.

Put a kid in some imaginary cliff-hanging situation, and nine times out of ten he'll figure out a pretty sharp solution. Here are some instantaneous reactions to the query: "What would you do if you saw a hungry lion coming down the street?"

☆

Boy: I'd run around and around until he got seasick, and when he threw up I'd escape.

☆

Girl: I'd tell him I was a lady lion and he'd fall in love with me.

☆

Boy: I'd tell him I was poison, and he'd leave me alone.

☆

Girl: I'd faint.
—Wouldn't he eat you then?
No, that wouldn't be fair.

And here's the solution to an ancient puzzle:

☆

Which came first, the chicken or the egg?
—The chicken.
How can you be sure?
—Because God couldn't lay an egg.

After some of the revelations on House Party, it's a wonder the kid has the nerve to go home. The other day I asked one small character what his father did for a living.

"He's an actor," he said brightly. "A TV actor."

"Really?" I said. "And what kind of parts does he play?"

"I don't know," he said sadly. "Most of 'em are so bad that Mom won't let us look!"

On that same program I asked a pig-tailed Miss if she was planning any New Year's resolutions.

"Well," she said, "I'm going to pray for peace."

"What's your idea of peace?" I wanted to know.

She heaved a small sigh. "It's when my dad gives in to my mother and she stops yelling."

I asked another demure young lady just who might be considered the boss in her house.

"My mother," she said instantly, "because she's the one who tells daddy where he can go!"

Talking to the kids before the show, I can usually tell which ones will be the liveliest and least inhibited when we're on the air. Sometimes, one will freeze up on me completely. When that happens, I just move on to the next. Sometimes, of course, the dialogue gets so fascinating that I hate to break it off myself. Here's a rapid-fire exchange I had the other day with a P.K. (preacher's kid):

What do you want to be when you grow up?
—A preacher.

Why?

—My dad's a preacher.

What does he do most of the time?

—He talks Christians into being Methodists.

Do you think he could get me into heaven?

—Sure, he'd just put you on a Methodist jet plane and shoot you there.

Where is it?

—It's about twenty miles past Mars.

What do you think it looks like?

—Everyone's lying around on big pink clouds eating angel food.

You have quite an imagination. Suppose a tiger came along and said he wanted to eat you.

—I'd put him on TV because he could talk.

What would you call the program?

—Me and the Talking Tiger.

That tiger would have a tough time getting a word in edgewise!

Glancing back over the files of various House Party programs, I came up with a double handful of staccato communiqués from the secret world of kids. Here they are, in no particular order, for your amusement, amazement, or delectation:

What does your dad do?

—He's a barber.

What's his main complaint about his job?

—Well, when he's cutting somebody's hair and the

phone rings, when he comes back he can't remember his place.

☆

What's the worst punishment your parents give you?
—Having a heart-to-heart talk with my dad.

☆

Do you want to get married?
—No.
Want to be a bachelor?
—No.
Then you won't venture into matrimony?
—I don't think so.
I'll bet you don't even know what matrimony is.
—Yes, I do. It's a dirty word.

☆

Any brothers or sisters?
—No.
Did you ask for one?
—Yes.
What did your mother say?
—Maybe in a month or so when dad gets rested up.

☆

What's the worst age to be?
—Somewhere between seven and nine.
Why is that?
—Well, you're stuck in school and you just begin to realize it.

☆

What do you think it's like in outer space?

—It's full of purple people with zigzag noses and orange eyes.

How do you get there?

—You go past heaven a little ways and then make a right turn.

☆

How do you think the Easter Bunny looks?

—It has long ears, a tail, and red eyes.

Where would its red eyes come from?

—Well, he stays up so late hiding the eggs.

☆

How would you define marriage?

—Boy: It's sort of like a cat springing at a mouse once it's cornered.

—Girl: It's something a girl does when she finally gets too old to do anything else.

How old is that?

—About twenty.

☆

What's the difference between a Governor and a Mayor?

—Well, a Governor must be a he horse, because a Mayor's a she.

☆

Young man, what's your idea of an ideal wife?

—It's some one who doesn't go home to her mother unless you want her to.

☆

How do you think people know when they're in love?
—It's sort of like heartburn.

☆

What does your dad do?
—He's a psychiatrist.
What's that?
—Somebody who helps you for a fee.
What's the hardest thing about it?
—To keep the most wonderful secrets in the world.

☆

What does your dad do?
—He's in the South Pole.
What's he doing down there?
—I don't know . . . I think he's drinking beer.
How long has he been away?
—Five years.
What's new at your house?
—I'm going to get a baby sister tomorrow.

☆

Did your parents tell you anything to say on the air?
—My dad told me not to tell you what he does.
Why not?
—Because it's a kind of funny word.
Well, suppose you just try for the fun of it.
—All right. He's a stupidvisor.

☆

Did your mother tell you anything to say?
—She told me not to say the truth about our friends.

☆

And what did your mother tell you not to say?
—That she's young, talented, and beautiful.
Well, is she?
—No.

When the kids are ten or eleven, I sometimes ask them more involved questions. The other day I asked my foursome to explain the difference between being young, middle-aged, and old. Here are the answers I got:

☆

—When you're young, you have school troubles. When you're middle aged, you have husband trouble. When you're old, you have heart trouble.

☆

—When you're young, you're in the way of your parents. When you're middle aged, you're in the way of your wife. When you're old, you're in everybody's way.

☆

—When you're young, you can stand on your head. When you're middle aged you know how to dance. When you're old you're laughing all the time because your whiskers tickle you.

☆

—When you're young, you learn all about school. When you're middle aged, all you do is worry about payments. When you're old, you're good for nothing but baby sitting.

☆

Another youngster had an answer that was more cynical, and shorter:

—When you're young, you get married. When you're old, you get divorced.

☆

Here's a moral code for young ladies in a handy, condensed version. I got it from a four-year-old:

What's your favorite story?
—Cinerwella.
What does it teach you?
—Not to go awound losing your clothes.

☆

When you live in the secret world of kids, history is pretty much whatever you care to make it. Here's proof:

Any instructions from home?
—Don't give any stupid answers.
Well, let's try you out. Who was the first President of the United States?
—Abraham Lincoln.
What happened at the Alamo?
—We lost Alaska.
When did we get it back?
—In World War I.
My advice to you is . . . don't go home!

Kids love to be asked what they're going to do when they're grown-up, and their answers often have a kind of demented logic. Here are just a few:

☆

What do you want to be?
—An arsheteck.
What's the most important thing to remember?
—To see that the house fits on the lot.

☆

What are you going to do when you grow up?
—Build houses.
How do you go about building one?
—You take a hammer and some nails and some boards and you hammer them all together, and if it doesn't fall down you've got a house.

Here's a practical soul speaking:

☆

What do you want to be?
—A fireman.
What if you saw a big fat lady up on the fifth floor who needed saving?
—I'd put a big ladder up and then get out of the way so I wouldn't be squashed if she fell down it.

The science of medicine fascinates a lot of kids, probably because so many of them have found themselves impaled on the business end of a hypodermic needle.

☆

What do you want to be?
—A doctor.

How will you go about that?

—When people come in, I'll ask them to sit down and let me see their germs.

What are you going to be?

—A trained nurse.

A nurse? That's fine. What do you know about proteins and carbohydrates?

—I don't know. I don't know which to vote for. Besides, I don't like politics.

Firemen and policemen always have an appeal. Maybe it's the uniform. Maybe it's the alluring prospect of violence or excitement. Some of the reasons that pop out are surprising, though:

What do you want to be?

—A fireman.

What's the hardest thing a fireman has to do?

—Getting his pants on frontwards while he's sliding down the pole backwards.

What about you, young man?

—I want to be a policeman.

What will you do all day?

—Pinch ladies until they stop.

One young fellow, though, said positively that he did not want to be a policeman.

"Why not?" I asked.

"Because," he said darkly, "you always get shot in the ending!"

Nothing delights an audience more than to see the rug pulled out from under the emcee. I won't forget this little lady in a hurry:

What do you want to be?
—Just a plain old housewife.
What kind of husband.
—Just a plain old man.
Well, give us an example of a plain old man.
—You.

So it goes, day after day, on House Party, and I could go on for page after page right here. But I won't, because there's really nothing to stop you from using this technique on your own kids. I don't hold any patent on it.

Try it tonight, at the supper table. Ask 'em what they'd wish for if they had just one wish. Or two wishes. Ask 'em what they'd do if they were in an airplane and the engine stopped in mid-air. Ask 'em what they'd say to a crocodile if they met one walking down the street. You won't get a gem of an answer every time, but I promise you that you'll have some fun—and so will the kids.

People ask me sometimes to pick out *the* darndest thing that a kid ever said to me. That's just about impossible. I think the one-word answer that impressed me most, though, in this atomic age, came from a kid who thought for a moment when I asked him what he wanted to be when he grew up and finally said: "Alive."

I told that one in *Kids Say the Darndest Things!* And I also told about the darling little girl whose shy answer to a question summed up for me all the magic and freshness and wonder of the secret world of kids.

"Have you ever been in love?" I asked her.

"No," she said, "but I've been in *like*."

Maybe that isn't my all-time favorite. But it'll do until a better one comes along.

Conclusion

"Our earth is degenerate in these latter days. Children no longer obey their parents. They show disrespect for elders, gobble up their food at the table, and tyrannize their teachers. The end of the world is near."

Who wrote that? A gloomy Egyptian priest, four thousand years ago, somewhere in the valley of the Nile.

Well, the end of the world is four thousand years closer now than it was then. But it hasn't happened yet. And in the meantime, I doubt if human nature has changed very much. We still have with us sour-pusses like our priestly friend who think that the younger generation has gone completely to the dogs. And we still have incurable optimists, like me, who think that kids are just about the most wonderful gadgets ever invented, and even stubbornly believe that they're getting better all the time.

Without this conviction, I couldn't have written this book, and I hope some of my optimism has rubbed off on you. As I said in the beginning, my main purpose was to open up a few channels of communication between the weary world of adults and the Secret World of Kids. To enjoy a child, you must understand him.

To understand him, you must communicate with him. What I've been trying to put on paper here is a blueprint for understanding and enjoying kids.

Whether I've succeeded or not, I would like to end by urging every parent who reads these lines to make a renewed effort to love and understand and appreciate his kids. It's terribly easy to take children—like good health—for granted. But they don't stay kids forever, you know. Overnight, it seems, they're grown up, they're gone, and then it's too late.

So don't put it off. If there's a trip you've been planning to take with the kids some day, *do it now if you possibly can*. If there's a certain book you've been meaning to get for your child, *get it*. If you've made good resolutions and have good intentions, *put them into action now*, before you lose the spirit of fun and play yourself, before the iron curtain of adult responsibility and routine clanks down and shuts you off forever from the Secret World of Kids.

Those of you who have kids of your own, stop for a minute and think about the wonder of it all: how these amazing little creatures came out of nowhere into your home, how eager they are for your attention and approval, how they give you the benefit of every doubt, how loyal and affectionate and responsive they are.

If once a day, for five seconds, you stop and consider what a fantastic privilege it is to bring life into the world and then help it grow, I think you'll be a better parent—and a better person.

Five seconds a day. If these words of mine can persuade you to do only that much, believe me, I'll be a very happy fellow.

Good-bye for now—and good luck to you and your kids.

THE END